NESTING

Tales of Life, Love, and Real Estate

LOIS WYSE

SIMON & SCHUSTER

SIMON & SCHUSTER
Rockefeller Center
1230 Avenue of the Americas
New York, NY 10020

Text copyright © 1999 by Garret Press, Inc.
Illustrations copyright © 1999 by Sally Mara Sturman

SIMON & SCHUSTER and colophon are
registered trademarks of Simon & Schuster, Inc.

Designed by Ruth Lee
Illustrations by Sally Mara Sturman

Manufactured in the United States of America

1   3   5   7   9   10   8   6   4   2

Library of Congress Cataloging-in-Publication Data
Wyse, Lois.
Nesting : tales of love, life, and real estate / Lois Wyse.
p.   cm.
1. United States—Social life and customs—20th century Fiction.
2. Real estate business—United States Fiction.   3. Home ownership—
United States Fiction.   4. House buying—United States Fiction.
5. Domestic fiction, American.   I. Title.
PS3573.Y74N47   1999
813'.54—dc21   99-37696
CIP
ISBN 0-684-84494-X (hardcover)

For

Phyllis Cerf Wagner

with love and appreciation—
for her friendship and counsel
and with thanks for the memories made
in the legendary nests she created.

Contents

Contents

FOREWORD

Who doesn't remember the start of it all, the days when we played house with a best friend, tested the waters, and tried to decide what life would be like when we made the rules?

It's a long road from playhouse to real house but, although few of us realized at the moment, our early make-believe was preparing us for the days of our nesting, the time when we would create a home of our own. In our first recollections home meant the place we'd find someone reaching out with open arms offering kisses to cure the bad and reward the good.

In our childhood homes we learned to make beds and memories, set tables, establish values, and practice ways to tame the wolves waiting outside our doors. For many of us, home always remains that first family address, and it is inextricably tied into feelings for mother, daddy, grandparents, caretakers, and siblings. Memories of home, no matter when we left, are always right under the surface, so that some disconnected event may suddenly propel us back into a long-forgotten place.

A sudden whiff of bread baking—or was that toast burning?—can erase the years and put us back in the first kitchen we remember. The sight of a single rose can make a garden of memory bloom. A cricket's chirp, an automobile horn, or a song on the radio let us live another life again. Just seeing a little girl in a plaid skirt, a boy hugging his dog, even hopscotch blocks chalked on a city street can conjure up a collage with images of home.

Like an involuntary reflex, the train of memory propels us from the present back into a half-remembered past. A familiar pull on the heartstrings, a rush of random emotions, and in a split second we are led back into the old familiar safety of the nest.

Inevitably those first memories become a part of our consciousness and subconscious and figure in our decisions, both positive and negative, about our own homes ("All I ever want is a flowered bedroom" or "I'll never have a flowered bedroom like the one I had"). Perhaps the reason each early nest echoes in some ways the one from which we flew is that the heart does not leave home with ease. It is hard to move on and move out, hard to know what will finally make us feel that our nest-in-waiting is indeed home. For many of us home won't be home until there's a spouse. For others a spouse isn't enough; there has to be a child, too. For a few it will be an absence of other people, rather than a presence, that makes a place feel like one's own. And for some it's home the day a dog or cat or goldfish moves in.

Some of us will never stop looking. Armed with recollections and hopes, we will go through life opening doors and looking for a place to call home, pausing first to get the beat of the place. Does this room talk to me? Can I imagine us here on a Sunday afternoon? Is this just another house or, wonder of wonders, does it feel like home, a sanctuary where dreams can be parked and fears hidden, a refuge where each of us can find the quiet time to heal both head and heart while coping with what is supposed to be real life?

We won't all love the same houses any more than we all love the same people. We don't all look at home through the same telescope.

Lois Wyse

One family's treasure goes into another's garage sale. But it is from treasures and not-quite treasures that we build and scrape to put together those bits and pieces of ourselves that make our nests.

This is a book about those nests we call home, the changes we make to find them, and the reasons we make them. We may repaint a house here or add a closet there, but in the world where ideas are traded, careers switched, and loves ended, what we are really making over is ourselves.

Each movement, each subtle alteration offers a lesson of life. While this is a book of stories, it is also a book about the lessons we learn as we go about finding a home for the heart, which is, after all, the true art of nesting.

NESTING

I *Memories Are Made of This*

WHERE'S ROBBIE?

The wallpaper in the nursery was purposely genderless so that both boy and girl babies (it turned out we had one of each) could live there. That's how it happened that Robbie, our second child, was born to live with deer on his walls in a Bambi-like world of green crib, green toy chest, and shaggy green grass carpet.

It was to this room that Robbie took his first playmates. In this sweet, protected space they sat on the floor and patty-caked as they looked out on a world of nearby houses and friendly neighbors.

By the time our son was two, he had grown (sort of) into a skinny little kid with an irrational appetite for orange juice, eggs, and not much else. Since his tastes were simple and his world seemed to revolve around one room, we didn't think it was necessary to have a long talk with him when we decided we'd move from the only home he'd ever known to a Bigger House. In the grand new house the children would have larger rooms; Rob would move from his safe crib to a big bed. He smiled and nodded. He understood that he was becoming a Big Boy.

We didn't bother to explain to the children (they were too young, we decided) that the larger home was on a heavily trafficked road opposite a campus with an elementary, junior high, and senior high school.

We moved in June, one of those poet's days when the sky was as blue as skies are supposed to be and the air so balmy that the words "air conditioning" never even came to mind.

The second day in our new house I opened all the doors to let the sunshine in, then put Rob and Kathy down for afternoon naps while I did what all of us do when we move—I unpacked more boxes. When Rob awakened after one of the world's shortest naps, he called me to dress him so he could "help Mommy." (Kathy, on the other hand, when awakened from a sleep, would ask, "Is I'm up?")

But Kathy wasn't up; she was still asleep when Rob and I went downstairs. Just then the telephone rang, and I took a quick call from someone who wanted to sell me a ticket for a charity luncheon. Then I turned around and went to see what Rob was doing.

"Robbie," I called. But there was no answer. "Rob,"

I tried once more. Still no response. "Honey—" Now my voice was getting a little frayed. "Robbie, Robbie, where are you?" I poked around the boxes. No Rob.

Where could this little kid be? Did he go out to the new, big backyard? Was he going to be some kind of explorer? Where was my junior Columbus? I ran out the door looking for him and calling his name. "Rob." Now I ran to the front door where cars were whizzing by. I had never been so frightened in all my life. Where was my baby?

I scooped Kathy from her bed, ran to the car, and told her, "I can't find Robbie. We have to go to look for him." As I swung the car out of the drive, Kathy piped, "It's too bad. He was a nice little boy."

"Kathy," I told her grimly. "He's not gone. He's just not here."

She didn't see the difference. At the moment I didn't either.

We rounded the corner past the athletic field. Still no sign of Rob. "Mommy," Kathy began, "should we sell his clothes or just give them away?"

"Kathy, we are keeping Robbie and his clothes. Now just look for him."

As we turned the next corner, we spotted him. There was Rob on the sidewalk with a woman who was talking to him. I rushed to his side and picked him up. "Mommy," he smiled. I started to cry. I couldn't speak, not even to the woman who was standing there. She turned to me. "I was driving past the athletic field, and I saw this little boy all alone. I assumed he was the new little boy on the street, but I couldn't figure how he came all this way alone. I knew no mother would want me to take him in my car, so I thought I'd just wait until you came to look for him."

It's been many years since that June day, and I still don't know how Robbie crossed that big street by himself and got all the way to the other side of the field. Nor does he.

All I know is that night when I tucked him into his bunk bed in his new room, I asked him why he went out alone. He blinked at his beige walls, looked down at the unfamiliar brown carpet, and said, "Because I was going home."

Home is not where the furniture is. And that's just the first lesson.

MOVING ON

It was not Lily's way to look back with long-ing. She regarded life as one long lesson in living. So why was she feeling so forlorn about the move she and Brewster were making? Certainly it was not a step backward. No, it was part of the forward thrust of their lives, their comfortable and mobile lives. The children were long grown, married, and grandchildren had been born. So why such sadness at leaving the big house and moving to the adorable old farm they'd found only two towns away? She wouldn't have to make new friends. Oh, she might have to change dry cleaners, but she could still come over to shop at her old greengrocer if she didn't like the new supermarket. But this move had filled her with a sense of sorrow that was foreign to her positive perspective on life.

Then one morning as she showered in her little

bathroom in the old house and counted the familiar square white tiles—just as she had for so many years, going all the way back to each of her five pregnancies—she felt the steamy water, the familiar, comforting presence of place, and knew the source of her sadness. She stepped from her shower, dried herself slowly, and said aloud, "I'm not going to be the mother anymore." With those words she knew she was relinquishing her life role. She was like the retired executive who wondered who would call once he left his office. She was the doctor who gave up his practice and missed his patients.

Of course that was the reason for this sadness. She had played the role of mother as if it were a starring part on Broadway. She had had a loyal costar—hadn't Brewster been that?—and the supporting cast of five children with their succession of playmates and friends, teachers and counselors. All of them had known that their home lives, perhaps their entire lives, revolved around the central life force of the house: Lily herself. Lily, the wife. Lily, the mother. Lily, the giver of life.

How can I leave it all, she wondered, and slowly she felt the warm tears on her cheeks. There will never be a place like this again, never a time like this, never a me like the one who is leaving. And no one knows how I feel. I cannot tell anyone, not even my oldest daughter, Melody, who is so much a part of my heart.

The movers came and went during the weeks that followed, and they seemed to move everything except the heaviness in Lily's heart. "Too hard to move that," she thought. The last day in the old house Lily stood at the kitchen counter and drank her last cup of coffee. "Mommy," she heard softly. She jumped although she recognized Melody's voice. "Mommy, I just dropped by because I think this is a hard day for you, and I have a present for you; but you have to come to my house to see it because you don't even have a television set here."

"And give up my last cup of coffee?" Lily asked petulantly.

"You'll be glad you came with me," Melody promised.

Lily was annoyed with herself. Why was she being so obviously depressed in front of her daughter? Her usual perkiness had been displaced for weeks by this bleak feeling.

"All right, Mommy," Melody instructed as she led her mother into the living room of her house. "Now sit back and relax. I want to show you something." Melody took a tape, put it in the VCR, and pushed "play."

Suddenly Lily sat upright. The camera was at the foot of the drive of the old house, and Melody's voice was leading her up the path to the house. And then for thirty minutes across the sweeping lawns and the greensward of memory, Melody recounted the life they had known. Who realized that Melody remembered the power outage ten years ago when Lily had lit a fire in every fireplace to keep them all warm (there were all the fireplaces, and Melody turning that tiny adventure into a comedy)? During the past weeks Lily had remembered the children only as perfect and dear. But here was Melody reminding her that there had been hard times in raising those children. "Look, Mommy, here are the back steps where Connie used to sit when you punished her with a 'time out.' Remember what she'd do? She'd hug her dog Ginger, that ugly little mutt, and sing 'Where Is Love?' the song from *Oliver!* that we all learned. And then you'd open the screen door and practically beg her to come back into the house."

There were the closets where the hockey sticks were kept, and the closets that held the first prom dress. "Remember the pink one, Mommy? All of us girls wore it eventually."

For thirty minutes Lily laughed and cried, and when the tape ended, she stood and embraced her daughter.

"I'm ready to move on," she said.

"Good," Melody smiled. "You see, Mommy, you can't say you weren't appreciated."

Lily dusted her hands briskly. "But I can't go back. I'm grateful for what I had, but now I know that I do want a next chapter; and I can't wait for it in the new house."

Houses come and go,
but memories remain.

New and Strange Streets

Emily parked two blocks from the building where the meeting was to be held. Lucky to get a parking space at all, she decided. But think of the long walk to the office!

She smiled ruefully. What would Grandpa say about a healthy woman who thought two blocks was a long distance? Well, Grandpa, she wanted to say, Just to show that I know what you're thinking, I'm going to go "by foot and by God," the way you used to say. I'm even going to go the long way, four whole blocks to the

south. She smiled. Kind of nice to be doing something because of Grandpa.

Sometimes Grandpa surprised her, came into her thoughts when she least expected him. Sort of the way he was. She wouldn't hear from him for a week, and then he'd call three days running. It was as if he knew when she needed him, needed his homespun wisdom for her city life. Grandpa had been gone three years now; still, his memory was a reassuring presence in her life.

Emily waited for the traffic light to change and then, true to her just-made promise to Grandpa, she went down an unknown street. It was one of those streets nobody notices because an office complex had risen around it. Still, like a cat that knew its home, it stayed. Probably filled with fusty old folks like her grandparents. I'll bet Grandpa wouldn't have sold to developers either, she mused.

Emily took the time to notice the row of pretty little houses, a bit down-at-the-heels, but still displaying the geranium pots and the promise of peonies. Grandma would have put her pots out by now just like the ones over—

Emily shook her head and smiled. Impossible. Or was it? There on a Florida street was her grandparents' home, or maybe its twin. Emily shut her eyes tight, just the way she had when she was a little girl and was waiting for a surprise. Then she opened her eyes and—surprise!—the house was still there.

The wonderful house where she stayed overnight with her grandparents when her mother and father were out of town. Grandma always said, "Bedtime, Emily." Then Grandpa would sneak up the back steps with cookies and milk, and the two of them would sit on her bed, like naughty children, and tell riddles. Of course, Grandma probably knew what they were doing. How smart of her, Emily thought. She let us have time with one another without interrupting.

But she'd had her Grandma secrets, too. There were the mornings she crawled into bed with Grandma, and her scratchy hands pretended to make biscuits for breakfast on Emily's back. How she loved those wrinkly hands.

And now there was Grandma and Grandpa's house.

How could this be their house though? I'm not in Mobile, but I am in the South; and when you see a house built up off the ground, you know you're in the Deep South. Oh, there's the space

under the house where my cousins and I used to hide our treasures. And there's the porch where we played Monopoly until it got too dark to see the play money.

Emily looked at the steps and took a deep breath. Dare she climb them? Before she could even consider the consequences she found herself at the front stoop and held her breath. What would she say if someone came out? No worry though. No one appeared. Emily waited a few minutes and then did what she knew she had to do. She climbed up on the ledge and peeked in the window, and she felt a small squeeze on her heart.

I thought Grandma had died and gone to heaven years ago. Maybe she died and went to Florida. Because this parlor is, I swear, exactly like Grandma's. Even the same old brass lamp on the table. Same over-stuffed Victorian sofa where Grandma used to make me rest when she thought I played too hard. Same curtains billowing at the windows. Same funny little footstool where Grandpa put his feet. And the strangest thing; there is even a loose pane of glass in one window, just like the loose pane at Grandma's. She used to ask my father to fix it, but somehow he never did. I must peek beyond the double doors to the din-

ing room to see if the little girl—me, of course—has put the telephone books on her chair so she can reach the table 'cause that's what I do just before I run upstairs to tell Grandpa to put his teeth in because it's time to eat.

Of course, I know this isn't Grandma's house. But isn't it just like Grandpa to send me down a street I'd never seen just to let me know he's watching over me still?

If you are open to love,
you will find old, familiar
messages from home, even if you
walk new and strange streets.

COUNT BY NUMBER

Gillian was still outside her apartment door fumbling for her keys when she heard the telephone ring. She gritted her teeth. Damn. Keys never worked easily when there was a ringing phone on the other side of the door. Finally—there—door open. Still time to get the phone. "Gillian here," she shouted breathlessly into the receiver.

"Darling." It was her mother's mellifluous voice. "Darling," she repeated. "No need to shout just because Daddy and I are in Paris. We can hear."

Gillian fell into the chintz armchair next to the phone. "Sorry," she mumbled. What was it about her mother that always made her feel that she'd made a mistake?

1437

"Just wanted you to be the first to know, Gillian dear. Daddy and I sold the house."

"The house, Mom? You mean our house in Detroit? How can you sell a house in Detroit when you're in Paris?"

"Well, you know that Daddy and I put the house up for sale before we left for this museum trip to Paris, and amazingly we just got a call from the real estate agent saying that the first people who looked at the house want to buy it at our price. So it's sold, and we wanted you to know."

"But what will we do?" Gillian caught herself. "No, I mean what will you do?" She didn't live in Detroit any longer. Her home was Chicago. Her older brother had moved to California and her younger brother was in medical school in Boston. Her parents had told her the house was for sale, but that wasn't the same as *selling* it.

"We're moving to that new condo they're putting up near the country club," her mother announced happily. "We're so excited; we feel like newlyweds."

"But what about us?" Gillian asked. "Where will we go for Thanksgiving? Is it big enough for the kind of Christmas tree we want?"

"Oh," her mother assured her, "you'll love it, too. Have to go now, darling. The tour is about to leave. Daddy sends you a big kiss, and so do I. I'll call you tomorrow about this time."

Gillian sat for a full five minutes. No family home? How could her parents do that to the family? No familiar ivy-covered walk to the red front door. No little garden where Gillian planted her first tomatoes and picked her first pansies. Gillian wasn't even married, but how could her parents be grandparents if they didn't have a family house? An apartment near the country club didn't sound like a home to Gillian.

At Thanksgiving the family met for their last dinner in what they now called "the house." Nobody called it home anymore.

"You children have to take your things from your room," her father said. "We can't move all your stuff along with our things of thirty-two years of marriage."

Gillian gathered a few of her childhood treasures: the teddy bear for the child she'd have one day, some of her favorite books. "Donate the rest," she told her mother bitterly.

"Good idea," her mother said with no trace of rancor. "It's silly to have so many things just stored with no one using them."

The next night, sitting in front of the fire in the living room after her parents had gone out, Gillian asked her brothers how they felt about this move.

"Hey, it's cool," her older brother said. "I'm glad Mom and Dad are still young enough to want to do things." Her younger brother was less enthusiastic but still supportive of the move.

"But what about us?" Gillian asked. "What will be home for us? There's only one 1437 Green Street."

"Hey," her younger brother said, "if that's what you think, ask Mom to give you the numbers from the front door, and then you'll have home wherever you go."

"What a great idea," Gillian said.

"You are really weird," her older brother said, shaking his head.

"And while you're at it," her younger brother said, "why don't you take the shelf over your bed, the one that all your friends signed when they came for pajama parties?"

"That's even weirder," her older brother answered, "but just to show I understand, I'll take it down for you, and you can take all that stuff back to Chicago and put it in your bedroom and pretend you're home."

And so she did.

Gillian packed her memories and put them on display in her studio apartment. At first she looked at them every day, but after a few months the pressures of her job—and the fun of a new boyfriend—made her forget about them.

The year passed quickly, and when Gillian's mother called to remind her she was expected home for Thanksgiving, Gillian demurred. "How can we be at home when you don't live at 1437?" she asked.

"Gillian, grow up," her mother commanded.

Gillian took a deep breath. "I am growing up, Mom. I have a new boyfriend. Really nice guy. May I bring him, too?"

"I'd like that, and so would your dad."

On Thanksgiving Day, Gillian, her parents, and her brothers, along with two stray cousins, a visiting aunt, and two friends of her parents, carved the Thanksgiving turkey at the same old dining room table in the new condo.

Gillian's boyfriend looked around at the contented faces, the laden table, and said loudly, "I would like to propose a toast to this family and offer my thanks for being in a wonderful home for this holiday. Thank you all very much."

And in that moment, through the eyes of a newcomer, Gillian saw it all.

Her mother had created the same kind of beautiful table that she had always offered at holiday time. There were the same loving faces. Only the location had changed.

Home isn't where
the house numbers go;
it's where the family goes.

SPRING CLEANING

Yes, I know.
You don't have to tell me.
There is too much in my house.

Last year's magazines . . . unread papers . . . unworn jackets . . . un-zippable skirts . . . unused pots . . . misshapen pans . . . keys to old doors . . . locks to forgotten secrets . . . a phone number with no name attached . . . two old telephones that don't work . . . four radios that don't play . . . a recipe that ends with the words "be sure to add" and nothing else . . . a typewriter with two missing keys . . . seven children's drawings . . . eighteen sea shells . . . hats piled in the corner of a guest room . . . 132 wire hangers from years of dry cleaning . . . a moth-eaten sweater . . . tablecloths I never use . . . towels I forgot to turn into wiping cloths . . . two chipped vases . . . three knives to be sharpened . . . an old fur

coat . . . four bathing suits I can't believe I ever wore . . . shoes I forgot to get resoled.

> *If you were to show me*
> *All those things in your house,*
> *I would say,*
> *"Throw them out. Throw them all out."*
>
> *But I will keep them.*
> *Because if I threw all these things*
> *From my house,*
> *It wouldn't be home.*

GHOST IN THE ATTIC

Mimi," Frank called from the kitchen, "I just read a real estate ad in *The Evening Sun,* and it sure sounds like our house."

From the bedroom they shared, Mimi called back, "You're right, Frank. It is our house. I put that ad in the paper."

Even before she could blot her lipstick Frank was standing in the doorway. "What's that about? You're advertising my grandpa and grandma's house, this very house where we live?"

Mimi turned, and there were tears in her eyes. "Sorry, Hon, but I can't put up with this any longer."

Frank didn't have to ask any questions. He knew what "this" meant.

After the birth of the twins, Frank and Mimi came to realize that they couldn't live in the little one-bedroom house they'd rented when they married. But times were tough, and landscape artists were not exactly what the world was fighting to hire. Still, Mimi wanted Frank to do what his heart dictated, and a few months later, just after Frank's grandmother died, his mother suggested they might want to move into Grandma Meadow's house. Want to move into a big, old-fashioned, roomy house? They both jumped at the chance.

"It's an old house, and Grandma wasn't much for decorating. I know that it needs some fixing up, but if a painter can't do something with it, who can?" Frank asked aloud.

So the young couple scrubbed and painted. They closed off the up-stairs rooms because they didn't need them, but two years later when

Mimi became pregnant again, they turned to one another delighted that another child didn't necessitate a move; now she and Frank knew that the upstairs rooms would be used. The twins were old enough to sleep on the second floor, and the new baby would take the downstairs nursery.

"Mimi, this time you don't have to do your dopey little decorations and homemade curtains," Frank said proudly. "And we can get rid of some of those old antimacassars of Grandma's and get that sofa recovered so it looks like today." His Andrew Wyeth–style was coming into vogue with a lot of young people, and his paintings were beginning to sell well. "We can afford to get some professionals," he laughed.

But Mimi didn't laugh. What was wrong with loving hands at home? Since when did Frank think that anything they bought was better than the things she and Grandma had made with their own hands?

Mimi knew that as an expectant mother, she was in no condition to do any of the major alterations, so she devoted part of each day to supervising the men Frank hired. "We need to move the staircase," she instructed them, "and that means we'll have to put in some new flooring upstairs and take down three walls."

Tim, the burly foreman on the job, walked through the house with her. "Great old beams," he smiled. "I love working in a house like this. Besides, I can remember this farm when I was a boy going to the school down the street."

"That's one of the best things about growing up in the town where you live," she agreed. "I not only remember the house. I remember Grandma Meadow. When Frank and I were engaged, she and I used to putter together in her kitchen, and she showed me how she made her apple pie. And I know it would make her so. . . ." Now Mimi's voice trailed. What had interrupted her sweet thought? A sound? No, it was less than a sound and more than a noise. It was a feeling, a sense of someone—no, not Tim—a sense of something, someone not of this world. Mimi reached out, but there was no one to touch.

"You're not going to faint, are you? What is it?" Tim asked. "I know my wife doesn't always feel so hot when she's—"

"No, no." Mimi clutched her throat. Something somewhere was—was what? Something was there. That was it. But nothing was there, and she knew it. "Tim," she asked breathlessly, "are there sort of—umm, kind of—dead spots in the house?"

He shook his head. "Not so far as I can see."

When Frank came home, Mimi whispered, "There's something going on in this house, something I can't explain."

"What do you mean?" he asked.

"I felt something or someone in the house today when Tim was here. He didn't feel it, but I did. It was almost as if it was a presence. And Frank," she began to cry, "it wasn't friendly."

He laughed. "Oh come on, Mimi. Voices? Are you sure that wasn't the new baby crying to be born?"

She looked at Frank and felt both hurt and anger well within her. Couldn't he understand that she wouldn't say something like that if she thought it meant nothing? "Frank, please don't make fun of me. I'm sure. I'm real sure I heard voices. Come with me."

She took him upstairs, and in the hall that had led to the old staircase, Mimi felt that thing again. But this time she wasn't alone in feeling a presence. Frank shuddered. "See," she whispered, "it's the *something*."

"Oh come on, Mimi," he said gruffly, "you're just making me nervous, too."

"Frank, you felt it. I know you did."

"Oh Mimi, it will go away just like morning sickness."

But it didn't go away.

During the next weeks of construction, two workmen left the job. "The house is haunted," one said. "I hear footsteps in that house even when I'm working alone."

Another could not open an unlocked door, and when the door was taken off, they found a steep drop to the first floor. "It's not a harmful ghost or whatever," he admitted. "I guess it even watched out for me. I could have been killed if that door had opened."

"It's the footsteps that get me," the first said. "I'm outta here."

"I know I'm pregnant, and I'm susceptible to all kinds of thoughts," Mimi admitted, "but Frank, this is getting to me. I'm going to investigate."

The next day Mimi went up to the attic. If there's anyone here, I will confront them, she decided. She trudged up the first six steps, took the bend, and there, sitting on the top step, she saw her.

She was wearing the familiar blue apron with the sprigs of white flowers, and she looked straight at Mimi. There was no mistaking her. Mimi had known only one person in the world who had one blue eye and one gray eye, and both eyes were fixed on Mimi; but that person was no longer in the world.

"Grandma," Mimi gasped.

Grandma shook her finger at Mimi and disappeared.

When Frank came home, she told him, "Frank, I know what our problem is. Grandma is in the attic, and she's angry that strangers are messing around her house. She doesn't know it's us, and you're not recognizing her so she's very annoyed."

"Now I know you're hallucinating," he snapped.

Mimi resolved to say no more, but all that night she lay awake listening to the footsteps overhead. The next morning she made up her mind; she had to act.

So she put the ad in the paper.

Frank had been standing silently in the doorway holding the paper folded to the page with the ad. "Maybe you're right, Mimi. Maybe we ought to sell the house."

Mimi nodded. "But before we do, I'm going to have to explain to Grandma what we're doing. She's going to be very angry if she doesn't understand, and then if someone tries to move in, she could be dangerous."

"Stop that nonsense, Mimi. Grandma is not in the attic."

"She has been all along, Frank. And I think I know what needs to be done. But I need you to help me."

Frank sighed.

"Just this once," she promised. "Give me one last chance with our ghost."

The next day Mimi called Hope, her best friend. "Get over here. I need you." Minutes later Hope had her arms around Mimi. "You're having the baby?"

"No," Mimi was grim. "Not today. Today your job is to stay downstairs, listen for the twins outside, and make sure nothing strange happens. I've called Frank at the studio, and he's going to come home and go upstairs right away. Don't let anyone else in the house."

Then Mimi went to her bedroom, took out a candle and Grandma's Bible. She waited quietly until Frank came home, and then she nodded soberly. "I'm ready to go upstairs."

Frank shook his head skeptically. "Okay, if that makes you happy."

"Take the Bible with your right hand, Frank, and hold my hand with your left."

He nodded and did as she asked.

Silently they moved to the stairwell and walked the creaking steps. As they rounded the bend, Mimi heard the noise. Grandma was stirring. Frank squeezed her hand. He'd heard it, too. Together they looked up, and there, at the top of the stairs, in the familiar apron, was Grandma.

"Grandma," Frank said hoarsely.

But this time Mimi greeted Grandma affectionately. "Oh, Grandma," Mimi called. "We've been wondering who's been in the house with us. We're so happy it's you watching over us. And now I know what's been bothering you. You were worried just because you didn't know who was messing around with your house. But Grandma, it's just us. Just Frank and me and our babies. We're all family. Look, Grandma, Frank is carrying your Bible just so you'll know it's us, your family. And now I'm going to light this candle so you can find your way wherever it is you want to go."

Bravely Mimi stood on the landing, Frank at her side with the Bible. Together they held the candle aloft. A minute later they felt a soft swishing motion, and the flame went out.

From the garden door Hope called upstairs. "Mimi, Mimi, there's a white light shining down your garden path."

Mimi smiled, certain that Grandma was following the white light, the light meant to lead her to Grandpa, perhaps even to her own parents.

"Good-bye, Grandma," Mimi whispered. "I promise we'll take good care of your farm."

"Grandma," Frank called to the retreating light, "now that you know it's us, we promise we'll stay and take good care of the farm. Your great-grandchildren will grow up here in your home."

*You have to confront
your ghosts in every home.*

MOVING THOUGHTS

Goodbye to giant steps
I took across these floors;
Farewell to walls that heard
The secret sorrows of my life.

I move now to a new world
And look down a varnished hall;
Who will take the first step
On this highly polished floor?

What history will be written
Once we close the door?

II Of Honeymoon Cottages,
Rotten First Apartments,
Mortgaged Mansions,
and That Secret Place in
the Heart We Call Home

THE MUSIC OF MY HEART

Holly lay watching the ceiling. There they were still, the three stars Todd painted in silver just above their bed the night she left college to come here to North Carolina to live with him.

Her parents, or what was left of an alcoholic father and angry mother, had raised no objections to her running off with this young man. But why would they? Holly was at college on a scholarship, waitressed at two restaurants, and didn't ask anybody for anything. She knew that she already had everything with Todd.

They'd met in an environmental studies class; the difference between Todd and the rest of the students in that course was that Todd was serious. Dead serious, he used to say, because we're killing the planet, and unless some people are dead serious about how we deal with garbage and pollution, there won't be anything worth saving.

At first she'd thought Todd was just another guy with a mission in life, a way to set himself apart. But she soon learned that the last thing Todd wanted was to be apart from the world; instead he wanted to be a part of the world around him. What she saw: a broad-shouldered, athletic, handsome, intelligent, totally dedicated young man who was the real stuff. But those weren't the distinguishing characteristics people mentioned first when Todd's name came into play. Instead they talked about the recent death of his mother and the subsequent inheritance that made him a multimillionaire. Holly couldn't understand why his gold impressed others more than his sterling qualities.

Holly, who'd lived most of her life in sandals and khakis totally unaware of money and position, saw always the man and not the money. When she and Todd fell in love, it was to the music of their hearts, not to the ring of a cash register.

"Do you want to marry me?" Todd had asked.

"Someday," she had answered. And then, with tears in her eyes, she whispered in his ear, "All I want is to have a home, a real home with you."

So Todd had bought this small rustic house nestled in the Blue Ridge Mountains. "We're not just going to be close to nature; we're going to be nature," Todd assured her. And for two years Holly lived her dream creating the first real home of her own with the only man she'd loved.

Then one day, as Todd had a routine examination—why was it just a routine examination, Holly wondered later; why hadn't there been bells and whistles to warn them?—doctors found "a suspicious mass."

"How can I save the world if I can't save the one I love?" Holly wondered.

"We'll buy time," Todd promised, "and we'll use our time to make even this beautiful world where we live more beautiful."

Each week delivery trucks arrived with new plants, rare species to be planted around the cabin. Months later, as Todd lay dying, Holly was planting new life around their home.

After Todd's death the plants and flowers and trees continued to arrive. With each shipment Holly felt again the wonder of Todd's love. Not only had he made plans for her, he had programmed, planned—and now she would plant—his dreams.

Now as she lay in bed, after a day of putting in the ground Todd's latest ideas for their land, she looked at the stars on the ceiling and thought, No, I am too full of feeling for Todd. Tonight painted stars are not enough. I want to see the real ones. She walked to the deck outside their bedroom and sat slowly in the rocker; leaned back to look up at the clear black sky, a velvet bed filled with stars; and suddenly she heard—what was that?—a tinkling sound. Bells. It had to be bells.

She ran from her chair in the direction of the grove of trees, and there on the branches above her head she could see little silver bells attached to the limbs. Tonight there was a soft wind floating the music of the bells through the air.

Oh, Todd, she whispered, so that's why you needed a ladder that last week. You gave me the stars, and now this. Her heart was so full she could not bear the weight of her feeling. Oh, Todd, she sobbed as she crumpled to the ground, the earth will never forget you. The plants, the trees will all keep growing because of you. You even left your music written on the wind.

It is fourteen years since Todd died. Holly still lives in the cabin. She never remarried. There was a boyfriend one year who was easily replaced by two dogs and a cat.

The plants and flowers Todd ordered continued to arrive for two years after his death and, of course, kept on growing. Now they are mature plantings. Each night Holly walks outside, looks up at the stars, and listens for her bells. "It is the music of my heart," she whispers, "and it reminds me there is still work we must do to keep saving our planet."

True love blooms
every season of life.

Monsters and Moguls

It was not a marriage made in heaven, and it came unraveled not with a whimper but with tabloid headlines that focused on money and a house in the suburbs. "He can have the money, but I want the house," Dominique told her attorneys.

"Let him have it," they advised. "It's only a house."

But they were attorneys, so how were they to know that it was not the furnishings of her house for which she fought but rather the furnishings of her life? Her heart and soul were in the house; how could she give him the place that identified her, not only to her friends and family, but to herself?

For seven years she had been the mistress of Larkspur. How could she

hand Stewart, that despicable, dreadful, deceitful—she couldn't think about him without feeling the anger boil within her.

"Rage is consuming you," her friends told her.

"I have a right to my rage," she answered emphatically. "Men like Stewart think they can take anything they want. They say I'll take the house, I'll take the wife young enough to be my daughter; let's just forget about the family I used to have. But I tell you that even if he gets the house, he will never be happy there."

But Dominique was wrong. Stewart did get the house, and he was as happy as any winner. He also got the young wife. Dominique ended up with a house in a community just ten minutes from Larkspur. That meant that all the neighbors knew—and read—the he-said-she-said details of the messy court battle and rumored infidelities that preceded the divorce. It was the kind of story that caused nervous ladies to lock up their husbands. Divorcées, especially ones with headline pasts, are not exactly a suburban housewife's delight. But one neighbor, Samantha, soon arrived, not only with the customary plant but a story to match Dominique's. "I know about your marriage, of

course. But I read it all through your eyes because my ex," she confessed, "was a monster husband."

"That's what I call my ex," Dominique said in surprise, "except that I add a few words. I called mine 'monster of the universe.'" With that the two women embraced, locked in the laughter of two survivors.

One year later Dominique's real estate agent called. "I thought I should tell you before you read it in the newspapers," she explained, "that your ex-husband and his new wife sold the house for $2 million dollars." She paused for a beat. "And he bought an even bigger one for $3 million."

Dominique did not know whether to laugh or cry. Of course he couldn't live there. A new wife could never live a life designed by a former wife.

An hour later Samantha knocked at the door. "You won't believe this, Dominique, but my monster has just sold my beloved house for more money than I ever dreamed. I made that house livable. I put on the additions, did all the gardens; now he sold it for $3 million dollars, and I'll never see a cent of that money."

"Wait a minute," Dominique said. She phoned her real estate

agent and came back to Samantha. "My dear," she announced, "your monster just sold his house to my monster."

"Perfect," Samantha said, grinning. "All my feelings as a first wife went into that home, so since my monster couldn't live there with his second wife, I promise your monster won't either."

People get the houses—and histories—they deserve.

The Most Beautiful House in the World

Carter never was the kind of rough-and-tumble little boy whose pockets were stuffed with muddy stones; his mother never had to scrub his grass-stained clothes.

His grandmother was perplexed by a child who didn't want to jump in puddles or play touch football with his cousins after family dinners. When she asked Carter why he stayed indoors, he shrugged, "But I like drawing. I like to build things with my blocks."

"Doesn't seem normal to me that a boy doesn't want to get his hands dirty," his grandmother mused.

As the years went by, Carter began to build even more complicated constructions. In between he would burrow deep in a chair to look through books with pictures of beautiful buildings. He could almost feel the unspoken elegance of symmetry and line as he looked at each.

No one was surprised when, at fifteen, Carter informed his family he wanted to be an architect. At the same time he promised that one day he would build the most beautiful house in Minneapolis.

"And who will live there?" his skeptical grandmother asked.

Carter smiled benignly. "I will, of course."

But it was a surprise to his family that Carter, who treasured beauty, fell in love with Maude, a plain young woman he met his freshman year at college. Further, Maude's tastes were as simple as Carter's were grand. Yet there was a radiance about this plain-looking young woman that touched Carter in much the same way as the beauty of buildings and tasteful furnishings. In her way she was a classic.

When Carter proposed to Maude, he promised, "I have a dream, Maude. Somewhere, sometime, I will build the most beautiful house in Minneapolis for us."

"I could be happy anywhere with you," she answered simply.

Success came easily to Carter. His talents were obvious, and he had more commissions than he could handle. "I design office buildings to make money; the houses are done for love," he told Maude. But what he never told her was that in each home he designed he held back just one idea, one small touch, that one day would go into his own dream house in Minneapolis.

All he told Maude of his grand plan was, "For the moment we're going to move to a small house you can manage easily. When I'm ready for the big move, I will tell you."

Maude nodded. Didn't he understand she had married him for the long haul and not the big move?

So Maude happily raised their two children in modest circumstances and, to keep herself busy when the children reached their teens, took a job selling sportswear at a small neighborhood dress shop.

"You don't have to do that," Carter reminded her.

"Oh, but I do," she answered. "I do this for my sanity, not my wallet."

Four years after their second child left for college, Carter came home and said, "I bought a lot today."

Maude nodded and put the meat loaf in the oven. Carter was in the business of buying lots. Usually he sold them to developers, and sometimes he bought a lot for a client who wanted him to design a particular kind of house.

Carter walked to the oven where Maude was standing. "Did you hear me? I said I bought a lot. But this one is for me."

She looked at him. "You?"

"Us really. It's time for my dream house. I can afford it. And now that I've found the lot, I'm ready to go."

Carter was not like any other person who designs and builds a home. He asked no questions; he had the answers. All his life he'd been headed for this time, this moment. He would not be rushed. He had the best client in the world, himself. It took six years for Carter to assemble the materials, build the house, and design the furniture.

Meanwhile local architects and builders began to speculate

about the look of the house. Workmen couldn't describe it to anyone; it was even beyond their comprehension. Besides, no one but Carter knew exactly what was going on at the site.

So, on that night six years after breaking ground, when Carter introduced his home to the community with a large open house to benefit a children's charity, people rushed for tickets.

Everyone expected elegance, but no one was prepared for the grandeur of the house. The adventure began when massive entry doors opened to reveal a circular foyer with a floor of green glass. Then fifty feet above the carefully crafted paneled walls was a dome of green glass. At each stop on the tour people paused to catch their breath.

From the circular concrete core, a grand staircase arched from wings attached to the cylinder. Who had ever seen a house like this? Who had ever seen seventeen-foot-high family rooms, interior shutters of Brazilian wood with perfectly matched veins, exterior shutters of stainless steel, and everything environmentally correct? Awestruck guests wandered through the three floors of living space to see the double-sided fireplaces in each room, the three security systems, two living rooms, and two guest wings. The pièce de résistance was the nine-car garage with its own turntable.

Between interviews and congratulations, Carter was so preoccupied that he didn't notice that Maude spent no time at his side that night. When the last guest left, Maude walked into the foyer and looked up. I feel as cold and distant as that green glass turret, she thought.

Later as they went to their bedroom with its two fireplaces, two baths, six closets, and small kitchen, Carter smiled. "What a night," he said to his wife.

Maude turned to him. "Yes, it's been quite a night, and before it's over I think I'd better tell you something, dear. I can't live here."

"Are you teasing me?"

"No, my darling. I've never been more serious."

"But why? Why wouldn't you love this? You've watched it go up every step of the way. You knew what it would be."

"But you never asked me if I wanted this, Carter. You told me that you did. Didn't you ever notice that I'm a simple woman with simple tastes? I don't want to live on a turntable like the cars. I want to live in a home."

"I've never really asked anything from you," he pleaded. "Give me a chance. This is my dream."

Maude sighed. "I've thought a lot about this, Carter. After all, I've had six years to think. I know what I'm going to suggest may sound peculiar, but listen. Let's live here for one year, and I promise that during the whole time I'll never say a word about the house; and at the end of the year, we'll see how I feel."

At the end of the year Maude went to see Carter at his office. "I think this is better said here than at the house," she began. Somehow she never could use the word "home" with that edifice. "Have you noticed that I can't even make meat loaf anymore? That wonderful kitchen has everything anyone would ever need, Carter. But it's—I just don't feel I can do anything normal and ordinary there."

"I know what you want to tell me, Maude. I've watched you all year."

"I've tried to like it. Really I have. But this house is bigger than both of us. I don't feel like myself. I feel as if I'm in a TV show. Nothing is me."

"I told you I know what you're going to say. And I don't want you to feel guilty. Look, you let me build my dream. And now it's your turn. Besides, honey, I think I have a client who wants it. We'll sell the house, Maude."

"I thought I'd have to persuade you," she said.

He shook his head. "I'm an architect. I design for clients. And you, dear Maude, have always been my most important client."

In the end they moved from the showplace of the Midwest back to the comfortable suburb where they'd raised their children, a place where a woman could make meat loaf every night of the week.

King-size love doesn't need six fireplaces in order to burn brightly.

In the Beginning

The phone was ringing when Kendall walked into the apartment, and she dove for it before the answering machine took over.

"Honey." It was Gary, darling sweet Gary. "I know we're supposed to meet tonight to pick out the wedding invitations, but—"

"You've changed your mind," she teased.

"Of course not. I'll never change my mind. I will love you forever, and don't ever forget that. This is something serious. Fred MacKenzie was my adviser when I was student teaching, and I just learned that he died two days ago. The funeral is

scheduled for tomorrow morning, but it's upstate; and I want to be there. I loved this guy, but if I go, I really should drive up tonight."

"But couldn't I go, too?"

"I wouldn't ask you."

"You didn't. I volunteered."

Gary was quiet on the long drive upstate, and Kendall honored his sadness by turning on the radio until she found some Debussy. "Okay?" she asked softly. He nodded and touched her arm appreciatively.

"All I know about the place we're going is that it's in the mountains," Gary said after one of their long silences. "I have a feeling it's someplace special though. Fred was a loving man. He had to have lived in a place he loved, one that loved him back."

"What a sweet thing to say," Kendall answered. "I hope we can live in a place like that someday."

"I guess I never thought about where we'd live quite that way. But that's what we all want, isn't it? Just to be loved back." Then Gary grew silent again.

She knew that he was holding his sadness in a small, private part of his heart, so she stayed silent, too, as they listened together to the music.

They stopped overnight at a motel on the highway and finished their drive the next morning. Kendall held the map and directed Gary to a small grove nestled between two mountain peaks. "Oh," Kendall gasped when they came at last to the shady place where a crowd was beginning to gather. "I've never seen anything so beautiful or peaceful."

Gary nodded, and hand in hand they walked to join the crowd.

As the small Quaker-like service began, Kendall expected Gary to sink even more into that silent place she respected and was afraid to touch. To her surprise, as speaker after speaker stood to celebrate the goodness of the teacher's life, Kendall could feel Gary's grief peel away, layer by layer.

Now, in contrast to the emptiness of the previous evening, Gary's spirits seemed to soar. And when Kendall stopped to examine her own feelings, she turned and said in surprise, "Gary, I'm filled with joy."

"That's because the people who spoke here gave us life; they didn't take it away," he offered as he sought the reason for his own uplifting sense of peace.

A good kind of place to make a home, Kendall thought to herself.

On the long drive home, Gary seemed more relaxed than Kendall had seen him in many weeks. She hadn't expected him to be so calm after such an emotional event.

"Kendall," Gary began, "does it sound crazy to you to think about living in a place like that?"

"I know you keep saying you want to leave the city someday. But now? How would we live?" Kendall asked.

Gary smiled. "We're both teachers; there ought to be something in the area for both of us."

"We could certainly investigate," Kendall said, and even as she spoke the words, she knew she liked the idea. "Gary," she said impetuously, "we don't have any plans next weekend, so why don't we just get in the car and come back up here? Maybe we should get a better sense of what it would be like to live there before we start looking for jobs."

"Good idea," he agreed.

The next weekend they came back and drove around the area. "Let's just say we'll browse the way we do in bookstores," Kendall suggested. But before long they realized that even though some places appealed to them from the outside, there was no way to see the interior of a house unless it was for sale.

"Let's stop at a real estate office and ask to see some listings," Gary said.

In the office Kendall pored over the book and looked at the pictures of houses putting their best facades forward. She turned the pages and shook her head. The prices were too steep or the houses too uninviting. Suddenly she pointed and urged, "Look at this."

"That's not even a picture of a house," Gary said squinting at the small photo. "You can only see a little bit."

"Oh, Gary, there's just something about the lattice work windows and the tree so close to the house that whispers, "This is it."

The real estate agent took them to the house at the end of the day and, as they got out of the car, they were all silenced by the beauty of a spectacular sunset at the foot of the mountains beyond the house. Before they opened the door, the agent reminded them that this house was a "handyman special," but after that sunset who cared?

Gary put his arm around Kendall, and she knew they had come home to a ramshackle house with two flowering quince trees in a mountain quarry.

They were married and went to live in the little village at the side of the mountain. Neighbors stopped by, and each added to the lore and legend of their home. They learned that Van Morrison had lived there while writing some of their favorite songs, and a photograph of the quarry wall was on one of his albums. They discovered that an eccentric had built the home as a honeymoon cottage and named it *Journey's End.*

In addition to wonderful, mystical things about the house, there were less-than-wonderful real problems. When they discovered, in addition to plumbing and heating problems, that the foundation was disintegrating, Kendall wrote to her mother, "It's nothing major; it's just that the house is falling apart, so we're going to put it together ourselves."

As the two mixed cement for the basement walls, together they recalled the name of every person who had supported their relationship, and they inscribed each name in the cement. They wrote Fred MacKenzie's name; the celebration of his life had brought them here. Other names—their parents, early friends, friends in common—began to fill the walls with Kendall's perfect calligraphy. Next they wrote their favorite words of wisdom, aphorisms, and philosophies to express their beliefs about the kind of life they wanted together. With ease they covered the entire sixty-foot area.

And then they plastered over the cement.

"Of course, no one will ever see those names and those words," Kendall said one night as she and Gary stood outside to watch yet another glorious sunset. "But we know they are there," she said softly.

He nodded. "Some people build houses; we built a marriage."

"From the basement up," she agreed.

*Every marriage needs
the right foundation.*

Short Play

The scene opens in the small but attractively furnished bedroom of a twenty-something husband and wife. It is obvious that they are a two-career couple. In the bedroom, in addition to the usual furniture, are side-by-side computers. Two briefcases are also open, and office documents are laying on chairs, table tops, dressers. The time is Sunday morning. Both are attractive, the kind of couple whose picture appears in the Sunday

style section when their marriage is announced. They are newly married.
HE is upwardly mobile, intense, good-looking; SHE matches him on all
levels and, in addition, is on a fast track on Madison Avenue.

Curtain opens at 9 A.M. on a Sunday morning one year after their
marriage. They are both in bed, drinking coffee, shuffling the Sunday
newspapers.

H E : *(puts down paper)* Do you think it's time for us to have a baby?
S H E : *(continues reading)* Job's too good. Let's build a house instead.

SCENE TWO

Same as Scene One, one year later.

S H E : *(puts down paper)* Baby now?
H E : *(continues reading)* Let's finish the house first.

SCENE THREE

*Decorator-designed bedroom in spacious home. There is no sign of com-
puters, office papers, etc. Time is Sunday morning, three years later. They
are served breakfast by a maid. When she leaves, he turns and speaks.*

H E : *(puts down paper)* Baby?
S H E : *(continues reading)* Yes.
H E : When?
S H E : *(puts down paper)* Now.

NESTING

SCENE FOUR

Same as Scene Three: Time is five years later, a Sunday morning. Both are putting on golf clothes.

HE: You kept the job.

SHE: We finished the house.

HE: So where's the baby?

SHE: We did it all. We have a beautiful house on a beautiful street in a beautiful suburb.

HE: And ten other beautiful houses with ten other golden couples sit on this same beautiful street.

SHE: And in all these years only two children have been born to the ten golden couples.

Never put the house before the
go-cart because it is easier
To make house than
To make baby.

A Man's Story

Pierre Arbot could solve any problem in his thriving electronics company, but a problem named Fiona had him flummoxed. Fiona was his beautiful, headstrong daughter who, at a marriageable age, managed to find only the most unsuitable of suitors, a collection of unemployed would-be philosophers, poets, and painters. That kind of romantic record was fine for a Paris student,

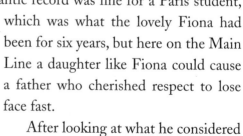

which was what the lovely Fiona had been for six years, but here on the Main Line a daughter like Fiona could cause a father who cherished respect to lose face fast.

After looking at what he considered the latest of the losers, Pierre decided to find a suitable husband. How would he hire a husband? Just the same way he hired executives. And since he'd already hired fine executive talent, why not look around his own company?

That was how Arbot came to have lunch with Edward Wilson one spring day. "Edward, you're doing fine at our company," Arbot assured him. "Now I have a different kind of job for you. You're not married, I hear."

"No, I'm not."

"Good."

Edward looked quizzically at his boss. Most people thought it peculiar that a thirtyish man was still single.

"Tell me about your family," Arbot urged.

"Almost nonexistent, sir. My parents are dead, and I was raised by my older sisters; so I feel as if I really had three mothers."

Arbot sniffed. No wonder the young man had good manners. Three women after him all the time. "Edward," Arbot said, "I have another job for you in addition to the one you have. You've seen my daughter Fiona?"

"Yes, sir. She's very beautiful."

"That's a good start. At least you like her looks. She's smart, too. A little too arty for me, but some people like that. Edward, I want you to distract Fiona. Get her mind off those worthless saps. She says no, but I'm sure she supports them all, buying their paintings and poems."

Edward, who'd never had a truly serious love interest, accepted the challenge. In truth the task was far from distasteful; Edward loved the theater and music and read a lot, so he had no difficulty communicating with and enjoying the company of the beautiful young woman. In time Edward found that Fiona filled him with a kind of mysterious joy he'd never known before. This must be love, he thought. Fiona, unaware at first of her father's interest in their relationship, found herself strangely attracted to Edward. Imagine! A real live businessman could be a friend of the arts.

After a courtship of convenience, Edward and Fiona married for love. For some years the marriage took its expected turns. Edward did well in the family business, succeeded Fiona's father, and eventually sold it for a price that made Fiona's family forever wealthy. Edward, of course, did well, too.

Not only did the marriage serve as the foundation for a comfortable lifestyle, it also produced two children. While he was a caring husband, Edward was an adoring father, and over the years he grew closer and closer to his children. And as that happened, he grew farther and farther from Fiona. She was a good mother, but her penchant for poet-philosophers had not ended with marriage; and now that she had money of her own, she was able to take an even more active role in the burgeoning art scene and a smaller role on the home front.

Still, Edward could scarcely believe it when, after ten years, Fiona told Edward she wanted a divorce. No amount of persuasion worked; she was determined to live her own life. So Edward, with a heavy heart, watched her leave. He agreed to the terms of the divorce. The children would live with Fiona, but he was distraught. How would they fare without his guidance? How would he get along without them in his life?

And that was how Edward came to make the decision that would guide the rest of his life.

"Hey, Eddie, want to meet some chicks?" a newly divorced man would ask.

Edward would feel instantly repelled. Chicks? After Fiona? Hardly.

So instead of the swinging bachelor life to which other men returned, Edward opted for the role of father. While there was no wife in his house, why could he not remain the paterfamilias?

Edward moved into a large apartment near the home where Fiona remained with the children. Edward would have visiting rights each week, so he hired a nanny and instructed her to run his home and help with his children. He still went to all the children's school functions, visited them at camp and later at college, and spent vacations with them. Even after Fiona remarried (a sculptor), Edward continued to have warm feelings toward the mother of his children.

Although Edward attended parties given by old and new friends, he did not see himself as part of a dating scene. Instead, whenever he was invited somewhere and asked to "bring somebody if you want," he would call any one of a number of interesting, unattached women and invite one to accompany him. They all knew one another and laughed fondly as they called themselves "Edward's women." They knew that he had no romantic interest in any of them. He would politely kiss them on the cheek when he arrived to take them out and said good-bye at the door. Occasionally, however, one or another of the women of the moment would decide she'd like to turn the moment into a lifetime commitment. Edward would firmly but gently explain that while the lady was in his Rolodex, marriage was not.

After the last of his children had graduated, Edward decided that the city apartment was no longer necessary. Now he wanted a home, a home where the weather was warm and the breezes balmy.

"You'll want one of those great condos in Florida," his friends said.

"Florida, yes; condo, no," Edward answered. "You see, I'm ready for a house, a real home."

Women raised their eyebrows suspiciously. "Why does he want a home?" The women who wondered were raised with the old shibboleth that men weren't homemakers but were merely tenants in their wives' houses. They believed the old joke that assured both sexes that women nest and men change channels.

But Edward did more than change channels. He also changed residences each season. After he bought the house in Florida, he liked having a home so much that he then bought a house in New England where he would spend his summers. Further, he hired a cook and maid to move each season with him.

His children are now grown and married, and he hosts them frequently at both his homes. His grandson comes to visit on vacations from college, and the list of ladies Edward accompanies to the opera, the ballet, dinner parties, and theater grows longer each year as divorce and death increase the population of available women.

Edward cannot imagine any other kind of life. He walks and bicycles every day, reads—always nonfiction, primarily biographies—and keeps up with his friends wherever they may live.

"Travel!" he scoffs. "No, not for me. My only traveling is between my houses. The places I've wanted to see I have visited over the years, and now I'm content just to stay in my own nests and watch all those other birds still flying around trying to find contentment."

Given the opportunity,
many a man would feather
his nest rather than take up
with a lot of strange birds.

LIGHTING THE WAY

Little Robin flew from the nest when she was three; Virginia enrolled her at the church nursery school just around the corner from their house.

"A Jewish child at a church preschool?" Sam had asked. "It doesn't make sense to me, Virginia."

"Don't worry," Virginia assured him. "She'll know she's Jewish soon enough."

But just after Thanksgiving, Robin came home and asked her mommy, "When are we going to get our Christmas tree?"

"We're not getting a Christmas tree, Robin," her mother explained. "Our holiday at this time of year is called Hanukkah, and I am going to tell you the story of the Hanukkah lights."

Robin liked the story, but then Robin liked all stories. What she particularly enjoyed was the promise that because the oil had lasted for eight days, children received presents for eight nights.

"Is that more than Christmas?" she wondered.

Now Virginia was troubled. "Sam," she said, "we live in a neighborhood where some families are Christian, some Jewish. We have other differences, too. There's a Greek Orthodox family on the next street, a Buddhist in Robin's class. I have an idea. . . ."

Virginia began with the six neighbors closest to her. "Come to our house for dessert next week," Virginia said, "and we'll each make something that symbolizes the holiday for our family. We'll make it a preholiday get-together."

The children loved cooking with their parents, and they brought Christmas cookies, potato pancakes, applesauce, and kuchen. Each child was excited to have friends taste the product of his or her kitchen.

Virginia urged them all to bring their desserts into the family room and sit together in a big circle. Then she showed them a dreidel and taught them how to spin it and play the Hanukkah game. She explained that their family was Jewish; they celebrated

Hanukkah, and she wanted each of them to know the story.

Virginia looked around at the upturned faces and said, "The reason I want all of you to know about us is that in our neighborhood a lot of different kinds of people live together. And this is what the world is about. In the next few weeks we are all going to celebrate holidays that are important to each family here. I just told you the Hanukkah story not because I want to tell you what makes us different. I want to tell you what these holidays have in common.

"The theme of both the Christian and Jewish holiday is light. We have Christmas lights because it was the Star of Bethlehem that lighted the way to the Christ child. And we have Hanukkah lights because the oil for the Eternal Light in the temple was meant to last for one night; and it lasted for eight days."

Now Susan, Virginia's next-door neighbor, picked up the theme. "And just as we celebrate the light of holy days, we must let that light guide us. All of us don't celebrate the same things in the same way, but we all celebrate the human spirit."

After the last guest left, Sam turned to his wife. "You just turned us into a true neighborhood. I think you made all of us understand that peace really begins in the home, not with a Santa Claus at the mall.

Virginia smiled. "Just wait till spring. I have even better ideas for Easter and Passover."

Nothing makes you more worldly than the lessons learned at home.

WAVES OF HAPPINESS

Kevin looked at the crumpled newspaper ad in his jeans pocket and let out a sigh. Conventional wisdom dictated that summer rentals in the Hamptons be negotiated in February. March 1 was practically the cutoff day for New Yorkers to find a place. So here he was, right on time, looking in February. Kevin trudged around cold, deserted beach houses, but the real estate experts admitted to Kevin that summertime bargains were about as rare as a July day in February.

"Even coffee is no deal," Kevin growled to himself as he walked into the diner. "Coffee," he said. "Hot and black. I want something to warm my hands." He took the paper cup out to the car, put it on the empty seat next to him, and drove to the beach feeling disappointed and downhearted. He didn't know if his anger and disappointment were directed at his own inadequate income or every real estate copywriter who promised a "bargain." All that he'd seen were houses with price tags meant for Wall Street bankers. Didn't anybody know that a single guy, a guy with a future, wanted a summer house that wasn't going to rent for more than he made in a year?

But he wasn't going to give up his summer dream. Not just yet. First he had to see the reason for the trip. Kevin drove almost by instinct on the now-empty road to the beach, parked on the gravel, and sat back hugging his warm coffee cup and looking out at the ocean. This was it, he told himself. This is what they meant by bargain. A beach for everyone, old or young, the richest and the least moneyed.

He got out of the car, almost without thinking, and started to walk on the sand. Cold, hard sand. Not at all like the sands of summer when bare feet dug into the warm and willing beach. And the sounds of summer were stilled in the February cold. No little children building sand castles. No dogs running and barking along the shore. No mothers shouting about who's hungry or thirsty. And no men hiding behind the *Wall Street Journal* and *Forbes* magazine. No beach like this one, he said silently. Now the cold was forgotten, and with the fresh salt air

filling his lungs, Kevin started to speed-walk
on the sand. Oh, this was good. He took off
his jacket and tied it around his waist. Sweat-
shirt was enough. Hey, why not? He was in
damned good shape. Went to the gym three
times a week, played a little squash, some tennis. And here he was at twenty-seven years of
age, a college graduate, restaurant manager,

mother-trained to be neat and clean and quiet. For the moment he almost forgot that he couldn't find a house to rent that he could afford.

Little by little he was aware that in the gentle lapping of the
waves he could hear his name. "Kevin. Kevin." He looked around
even though he knew the mind could play strange tricks on the
beach. And then he saw her—a girl, no a woman, and she was wav-
ing at him. So it wasn't the waves, after all. "Kevin," she repeated as
she ran toward him. "Kevin, I've been calling out to you. I spotted
you back there and ran down to see you." She paused. "I can tell you
don't remember me. I'm Alana Brown. I met you at the Packards',
you know, their Christmas party. We shared a cab."

"Oh, I remember now. You were there with—"

"No names, please. That's over. What are you doing here on the
beach? Do you have a house out here?"

He laughed. "Well, that's my dream. So Alana, do you want to share another cab or shall we walk together?"

"Walking is all I can afford," she responded. "I'm out looking for a summer rental, and I can't believe these prices. So I came down to the beach to see—

"—me," he finished. "Obviously you were looking for me."

She nodded. "Of course. Aren't you a gazillionaire who wants to buy me a little old place on the oceanside?"

He laughed again. "Not until I know you better."

B ack in the diner they exchanged the usual New York vital statistics. She was twenty-eight, an art director at an advertising agency with dreams of being a painter, just out of a long-term relationship with her college boyfriend, shared a downtown loft with three other women.

He was going to own a restaurant some day, lived alone, had no relationship, liked women, and loved men.

Just before she ordered her second cup of coffee, Alana asked, "You a neat, clean guy?"

"Very."

"Okay." She shrugged her shoulders, paused a minute, then said,

"Since we know each other so well, how would you feel about sharing a house? Bedroom for each of us, guest room, and we'll take turns having guests. Together we can probably scrape up enough for a decent place. And," she paused to sweep her arm across the narrow coffee shop, "we could stop meeting like this."

Four years and three rental houses later, Kevin and Alana had to admit they were a good pair of housemates indeed.

They had each given private space to the other and had been considerate of each other's guests. They confided in each other, adjusted their life habits (she slept late, he rose early and made the coffee). They did their summer entertaining together and occasionally the two had dinner in the city. Each January they breakfasted together to budget for their rented summer house and review their options. In February the hunt began.

And then, in the mid-nineties, Kevin said as they sat down to their usual first-of-the-year breakfast, "I'd like us to buy a house together."

Alana looked up. "Hey, I almost spilled my latte on that one. But if we can afford it, why not?"

"Okay then, let's look for something to buy this February," Kevin said decisively. "I'm going to St. Barts next week for a little sunshine because I worked all through the holidays; and I'm pretty tired. But I'll call you when I get back, and we'll see what's out there."

They lifted their bagels, toasting the New Year and their new decision.

Lying on the beach in St. Barts, Kevin turned and greeted the newly arrived couple in the chaises next to him, and they exchanged typical tourist small talk. After a few minutes the man looked closely at Kevin and asked, "Have we ever met? I have a feeling my wife and I have seen you before. We have a house on the Island. Do you by chance have a house at the beach?"

"Sort of. I'm a renter. But now that you've said that, I think I recognize you, too. Do you live just around the corner from the church in that terrific house—"

"Not just one house," the man answered. "We have two. I just bought the lot next to me to build a tennis court. There's a house on that land, and I'm going to raze it."

Kevin almost fell off his chaise. "I know that house," he gasped. "Listen, don't raze that house. I tell you I know that house. It's a perfect small house. I run every morning, and I run down your street and past that house. Please, sell that house. Sell it to my housemate and me."

"You'd have to find a piece of land, move the house—"

"Whatever it takes. I know Alana will agree."

It was not easy finding the land. The first piece of property they saw couldn't fit the house.

The next piece had problematic water.

Seven other lots had eight other problems.

Finally they found land and began, at last, the process of disassembling and moving their house.

In six pieces the little Greek Revival house was loaded on a truck and carefully moved the four blocks from where it had stood for years.

Architects, contractors, plumbers, and painters took up the better part of a year assembling the house. And each week the two housemates met to review the progress.

"What about colors and fabrics?" Alana asked Kevin one night when they met for dinner.

"Let's go through magazines and each bring what we like next week when we have dinner," he suggested.

She agreed. The following week each brought a sheaf of magazine clippings. They traded folders, and both burst out laughing.

"Do you realize we cut out exactly the same pictures from magazines?" Alana gasped.

"Now you know why we get along so well," Kevin said.

"You know, Kevin, for a long time after we decided to do this I was afraid to think about it too much. It's costing so much money, and I thought it didn't make sense. But I'm learning that this venture isn't just about a house, and it isn't just about our friendship. This is about finding a real home. I haven't felt a sense of home ever since I left my parents and went to college. I'm past the point of feeling my mother is where my home is. I love my sisters, but I'm not at home in their houses. I'm not married now, so it's not a man who'll make me feel at home. Only a house can make me feel I belong in the world. I'm grateful we can do this. Sometimes I cry with joy at the thought of it all."

Kevin nodded his head in agreement. "When I was growing up, I thought a house was about a man and a wife. But it's not. A house is about where each of us goes to discover a self. This is the freest thing I've ever done, which is kind of strange considering it's the biggest obligation I've ever made."

On the fifth anniversary of their joint tenancy, Kevin brought a bottle of champagne out to the house.

"To my housemate. To my house," he toasted.

"To my life," she responded.

Sometimes houses, like dreams, can be wheeled into place.

JUST A HOUSE

It was a door-slamming, screaming departure, and Heather still doesn't remember who said the *D* word first. But one thing she couldn't forget. She was getting a divorce.

There was the customary lawyer hassle, the he-said-she-said stuff, and after eight years of marriage, Heather was left with a little six-year-old boy, a big mortgage, and small help in keeping up either. "But," as Heather told her mother, "I'm not trading Billy, so that means this house will have to go."

The new house was a lot smaller than the old one, and so was the mortgage. As Heather put her pots and pans in the kitchen, she realized that Billy was sitting forlornly in a corner next to the window. Heather stopped and looked at her son, and her eyes filled with tears. She wanted so much for him to feel good about this new home.

"Want to make some fudge?" she chirped.

"You never made fudge before," her son mumbled.

"Mmmm, I think there's a recipe on the chocolate box."

"Don't care if there is. I hate fudge."

"Then how about playing outside?"

"There's nobody to play with."

"Look, see those boys in the next yard—" her voice trailed off. Of course Billy saw those boys. That's why he looked so sad. They were having a good time together, and Billy was on the outside.

"Let me take you over there," Heather said impulsively. "Come on," she urged her son, "you know if you meet people you'll really like our new house."

Billy made a face at his mother. Couldn't she understand a kid didn't want his mom to look for friends? Didn't she know that she was making him feel even dorkier? Besides, this was just a house. Why did he have to like it?

"Well, I guess we'll try another day," Heather said bravely. "See? One of those boys has to go home. That's probably his mother on the back porch calling him now."

Billy did not answer. He just pressed his nose against the window. Heather longed to put her arm around her son, but she held back. Instead, like her son, she was riveted by the scene across the shrubs. That mother looks youngish like me, Heather thought. Oh Billy, she longed to say, I want a friend, too.

Billy and Heather watched wordlessly as the mother spoke to her son, patted him on the head, and went back into her house. But the boy, instead of returning to play, walked through the hedges to—

"Here, he's coming here," Heather whispered as if the sound of her voice might break the spell. Oh bless that

mother who understood the heart of a new little boy in the neighborhood.

The doorbell rang, and Billy looked at his mother shyly. "I'll go to the door with you," Heather said.

"My mom is making cookies," the boy announced.

But he didn't add, "Want some?" Instead the boy blurted, "Can Mom borrow a cup of sugar? As soon as she finishes, she's going to the store, and she'll get it back to you."

It's a start, Heather assured herself as she ran to the kitchen, grabbed a two-pound bag, and handed it to the boy. "Take it all," she said, "and give it to your mother. This is Billy—" But before she could finish, the boy was jumping over the hedge, sugar bag in hand. Billy stood numbly at the door.

"Don't worry," Heather said confidently. "He'll be back."

Sure enough, less than a minute later the bell rang, and the boy was at the door with the very same bag of sugar.

"Didn't she want it?" Heather asked.

"Yeah," said the new neighbor, "but my mom didn't want your sugar. I was supposed to go to the neighbor's house, but you're not our neighbor. They moved away. Our neighbor is on the other side, so here's your sugar."

Heather took the two-pound bag. It felt like a fifty-pound sack. She turned. Billy had already gone to his room.

Heather took a deep breath. Okay, she decided. I may be brave enough to watch a husband walk away, but I'm not brave enough to let my son lose a friend he doesn't even have.

Heather's tennis shoes made a crunching sound as she crossed the driveway into the postage stamp yard of the boy next door. She walked up the back steps and rang the bell. "I'm Heather, your new neighbor," she announced. "I know you're baking cookies today, and I came to see if I might help."

"Help?" the neighbor echoed. "I'm trying to get my son's sixth birthday party together, put dinner on the table, listen for the baby, and take care of my sick mother. You're the first person in ten years who ever asked to help me. Come right in."

"I also have a six-year-old son," Heather said softly.

"Why, I didn't know that. To tell the truth, I've been so rushed I didn't even notice the day you moved in. And then I was too busy to go to meet you. Oh, please accept my apology. Honestly, we have a really friendly neighborhood. You and your son have to come to the birthday party today. He'll meet all the kids, and you'll get to meet the moms. Bring your son over now, and he can help the kids get the games together for the party."

"I'll get him now," Heather said quickly. "He's at the house. I mean he's at home."

Real estate makes houses; neighbors make homes.

TIFFANY AT HOME

No, Mrs. North isn't here. This is her daughter Tiffany . . . oh Gregory . . . sure I remember you. We were both in that psychology lab our last semester at college. And you just happen to be in town? What are you doing here? Oh, funny. You're here for a conference at the convention center, and you thought you were calling my mom to find my phone number; and instead you got me. Well, sure you got me. This is where I live. What do you mean, why am I living with my parents? Have you ever tried to rent an apartment in this town? Not to be believed. It's just big money for a little space that's too disgusting to even talk about. So after I looked and looked—hey, I even tried rooming with one of the women at work, and she was

NESTING

really bad. Such a slob, and she wanted me to pay for everything. So I talked it over with my parents, and they said, 'Look, we still have our house. Why don't you come back here?'

"... No privacy? Who are you kidding? My parents are so cool. Besides, they travel a lot, and when they're here, they have their life. So I live here, get my meals and laundry.

"... My social life? Better than ever. Everybody I know is so tired of frozen dinners that they practically die for invitations to come to my house. My mom still cooks dinner a couple of times a week, so if you want the best food in town, come here tomorrow night. I think we're having osso buco."

In life, as in poker,
a full house wins.

DESTINY

I can't believe it," Diane said to the real estate agent. "Here's a house that lives up to the advertising."

"Yes," he nodded sagely and then said, as he must have so many times before, "You know it was Mark Twain who said that many a small thing has been made large by the right advertising. But this house didn't need any words to magnify its worth."

Diane nodded in agreement. "All right, I'll take a deep breath. But don't tell me the price. Write it on a piece of paper, show it to me, and I'll faint quietly in a corner."

He shrugged, "Well, if that's what you want, that's what you'll get." He took out a small ballpoint pen and pad, wrote a number, and handed it to Diane.

She looked at him, laughed, and tore up the paper. "When the house is reduced to half this price, call me," she said.

But the call didn't come. Instead another family met the asking price.

Diane put the house out of her path of dreams. "What's the use?" she asked her sister. "Somebody actually paid the price. You know, it doesn't matter that I'm a single woman with a big income and a hot career. There just comes a time when you have to say no. This was that time for me."

So Diane continued to rent the house where she lived.

Two years later the real estate agent called. "Your dream house is for sale—again," he half-whispered.

"Don't tease me," she responded sternly. "I can't deal in disappointment again."

"In case you haven't noticed," the agent informed her, "the real estate market out here has dropped dramatically—

"—I stopped looking—"

"—and now you can buy your house for half what it was offered two years ago. The family who bought it has been transferred to Europe and needs to sell fast. If they can move in thirty days, they have all kinds of tax advantages and—well, do you want to see it?"

Thirty days later Diane moved into her dream house.

She reveled in the beauty of the place, and she marveled that each day she never tired of the view from her living room and her bedroom across the pristine pond into an endless wood on the other side.

And then one day Diane awakened, rushed to her window to see the view she now called hers, and let out a shrill scream. "The woods," she cried. "The woods. Where are they?"

Indeed the trees had been chopped, and instead of the deep and cool woods she loved, Diane was now looking straight into the picture window of a house across the pond. She called the real estate agent. "How could they do this?" she asked.

The real estate agent paused. "I told them you wouldn't like it, but I couldn't stop them. It's their property. You see, the people who live in that house want to sell, and everyone who comes to see the house asks, 'Isn't there supposed to be a water view?' I've told you it's a slow market now, so they did what they thought they had to do; they cut down the trees for the water view."

"But when people look at that house, they won't have the kind of water view we all want. They'll be looking right into my house." "I know," he said sadly.

The next week Diane went to London, where she met with a woman psychic represented by her talent agency. Diane, a crisp and efficient executive, was not much impressed by the idea of a psychic; but the two had time together, and Diane was floored by the psychic's ability to know and understand all the important people in Diane's life.

"When you come to the States next month," Diane said impulsively, "you must stay with me at my house."

The next month, when she arrived in the States, she went directly to Diane's house. It was nighttime, so Diane did not have to explain the dreary view from the window. Instead she showed the house she loved.

"How beautiful," the psychic said.

"I must tell you one thing," Diane admitted. "When you wake up in the morning, you'll be disappointed because the view from the living room is terrible." And she explained what had happened.

The psychic turned to Diane. "Take me to that window again." She retraced her steps, stood before the large picture window, and said quietly, "But I see nothing there."

"No," Diane said, "you can't really see the view from here now, but in the morning you'll understand when you see that other house—"

"No," the psychic answered, "I don't think you understand. There is nothing there. There is no house. It is gone."

"Gone? But how? Fire? What?" Diane asked.

"I don't know," the psychic answered.

Two days later Diane had a phone call. "I am your neighbor across the pond, and I understand that you are upset by the trees we took down. I wanted to tell you that we've been trying to sell our house for months, and no one wants it because your house, not the pond, is the view. So, if you'd like, we'll consider selling our property to you."

Days later, the deal concluded, Diane called the psychic who was now back in London. "You were right," Diane acknowledged. "There's nothing there across the pond. I bought the house, razed it, and my view is there for eternity."

Every house has a destiny,
but even destiny can
use a helping hand.

ALL THE HOUSES IN THE WORLD

Morgan and Martha married the month after he came back from service in World War II, got his first job, and proudly showed her his first week's paycheck; it was fifty dollars.

"I'm going to make my first million before I'm thirty," he promised her.

She shook her head. "I'll be satisfied if you make ten thousand dollars a year," she said to him.

Both spoke the truth.

He not only made his first million by twenty; he made his first billion by fifty and established a charitable trust before he was sixty. Martha, pleased but not inflated by his success, was interested chiefly in raising their three sons and later participating in the family trust to help support her interest in education and the arts.

Along the way the family, as it increased its size and wealth, also increased its real estate holdings. The house in the suburbs remained the focus of what Martha called home, but she knew they always had at their disposal an apartment in New York, a vacation retreat on the lake fifty miles from their home, as well as a winter house in the Caribbean. Then one evening as they were dressing for yet another formal dinner, Morgan told Martha he thought they ought to consider buying a vineyard in Italy.

But instead of responding with her usual enthusiasm, Martha turned to her husband. "I feel tired. Let's talk later, Morgan," she whispered. Then Martha went into her dressing room, lay down on a small sofa, and died peacefully.

Months later Morgan was as distraught as the day Martha died. "I've never been alone," he told his sons. "How could Martha do this to me?"

"She didn't do this to you, Dad," his eldest explained. "Life did this to both of you. Nothing is forever."

"Easy to say when you don't really believe it," his father mused sadly.

His daughter-in-law was more practical; she had more than advice to offer. "Come to the opera benefit with us, Morgan," she said. "I have a friend—"

The friend turned out to be a longtime widow, a woman Morgan and Martha had known, but not one with whom they had been particularly friendly. Morgan, lonely and sorry for himself, fell in love with her that night. The next morning he told his daughter-in-law.

"Whoa," she said. "Morgan, you're just out in real life for the first time in fifty years. You can't fall in love like that."

Morgan, unused to anyone telling him what he could or couldn't do, snorted, "Yes, I can."

Over the next months he became the widow's steady escort at the ballet, the symphony, the theater. When she mentioned casually that she was soliciting money for a new ballet troupe, he said, "Stop at once. I'll give you whatever you need."

When she mentioned her involvement in Meals on Wheels, he underwrote the entire program for the winter.

When he offered to give all the money needed to build a school for dyslexic children, he also suggested he name it for her. "And speaking of names, how about taking mine?" he asked.

"What does that mean?" she asked, accustomed to businessmen and their version of a deal.

"It means I want to marry you."

"I have been a widow for thirteen years. I'm not sure I remember how to be married," she said softly. "I just don't think of myself as a wife. I'll have to think about this." Then she added quickly, "But I am honored, so honored."

The next night his entreaty continued. "Marry me, and I'll give you—" he began.

"But I'm not sure I can be married," she repeated. "My dear, this isn't about money; it's about timing."

"But I'm lonely," he said sadly. "I was happily married for so many years and like a woman in my home."

"But you don't even know if I can be that woman."

Morgan had always been a strong negotiator. The harder he fought to make a deal, the more he wanted it. This widow, famous in her own right, would be his biggest win; after all, he didn't need another company to add to his portfolio. What he needed was another wife to add to his portico. "All right," he said with a wave of his hand, "I'll make a deal with you. Just come and spend a weekend in the guest cottage at my home in the Caribbean. Just spend one weekend and see if this isn't really the life you want. See if being my wife isn't the best thing that could happen to you now."

"A weekend?" she smiled at his self-confidence. "Why not?"

"You'll have a beach to yourself, so bring books. Servants are there, so we never have to go out to dinner. Martha and I loved being there."

The widow nodded. Who knew what might happen? Perhaps this was the life she wanted without even realizing that she might have it.

The first day Morgan apologized. "It never rains here," he began. "I don't understand this."

"Your cook said it's been like this for three days," the widow replied and then added, with just a hint of provocation in her voice, "But we're not really here to check the weather." She gave him her most beguiling smile.

"No, you're right. Weather be damned. Besides, I'm going to be on the phone with the office, so it's a good thing you've brought some books."

She nodded and went to her room. So much for her first attempt at a romantic response. She wondered what her three-year-old granddaughter was doing at this moment. If she were at home, she'd have the little girl with her because it was Saturday. But perhaps his concentration on business was just his style; maybe it had nothing to do with her. She'd try harder. When she came to dinner, she was wearing a long red caftan; her hair was pulled back, and she was wearing long earrings.

"You are so beautiful," he said. "Thank you for coming."

She smiled demurely.

"How did you spend your afternoon?" he asked.

"I did something I've been meaning to do. I finally had the time to begin reading the new Roosevelt biography. There were some things in it I'd never realized about—"

"Just a minute, dear," he said. "I think there's a fax coming through."

The widow looked around the pretty dining room and realized she had no one to talk to.

At the end of the second day, another wet day he spent on the telephone with his broker and at his fax machine, she realized for the first time in many years that she felt lonely. By herself in her apartment she'd always sensed the presence of friends and family. Here she was isolated with a man wedded to his business and the people who worked for him.

At dinner the third evening he had his finest champagne served, raised his glass, and asked, "Now are you ready to make this your life?"

"You are such a fine man," she began as she raised her glass. "I wish I could say yes to you, but—"

"Look at all I can give you," he interrupted. He looked closely at her. "I think we're compatible. We share the same values. I'm as devoted to worthwhile causes as you are." Now he set his glass down and put his hands on the table, the gesture he always made before announcing his best offer. "I'll give you thousands of dollars every month just for a clothing allowance."

She smiled sweetly. "That sounds like clamshells to me. I can't even translate that into how many dresses it would buy."

Now he pressed his hands into the table. "You can have all the money you want for charity. You'll have four houses, more if you want."

She shook her head. "Morgan, sitting in that little cottage, pretty as it is, made me realize that I felt very lonely. You have your computers and companies, but I want more than reading alone in a lovely place. Besides, loneliness isn't about being alone; it's about feeling alone."

She stood and walked around the table to where he sat. She kissed him gently on the cheek. "I'm going to leave tomorrow."

When Morgan returned to the city, he asked his second son for a list of eligible women, and three months later he announced his engagement to the widowed mother of one of his daughters-in-law.

Said the widow who spurned him, "I wish only the best for him, and I do hope his new wife will like me. He is a wonderful, generous man, even though he couldn't understand my decision. But you see, when a woman's been alone as I have, has learned to make a life for herself, likes nothing better than good conversation with bright and interesting people, how can she exchange it all for a rich man with a fax machine in all the houses in the world?"

Love is about the number of hours, not the number of houses, a man will share.

A Scene of Changes

She changed her name to Fred the morning of her thirty-fifth birthday. "I need to do something different," she explained when she phoned her best friend, Victoria. "I am getting nowhere with Mary. Frederica is my middle name, so why not use it? That name has just been sitting around on my birth certificate. It's time to try it on for size, and as long as I'm just trying, why not see if I can change my luck with a man's name?"

"The name is not the game," Victoria answered.

"But the only players in the game are named Fred or Joe or Bill. How many straight men who want to be married are still single at thirty-five? My biological clock is on eastern standard time and my life is three hours behind on Pacific time. At this rate I will never get married or have a baby."

"Is that so bad?" Victoria wondered.

"Maybe not for you," the newly minted Fred answered. "But I've got my body in pretty good shape for someone who lives on yogurt and take-out salads. I hang out at the gym because Mimzy—remember Mimzy?—met her new husband on the treadmill next to hers. I put in enough miles for cross-country expertise on that damned treadmill, and the only men next to me are potbellied guys getting over heart attacks or other women's husbands who don't want to leave home. No matter where I look, the only thing I see is a million other women like me. I see them in the deli and the take-out store. I see them at my office, in the movies, and on the bus. I'm damned tired of going home at night and wondering which *Seinfeld* episode they'll replay tonight."

"Maybe if you fixed up your apartment, you'd feel better," Victoria advised.

"That's what I said before I fixed up myself," Fred answered. "But if a new body didn't bring the boys around, why will a new sofa?"

"Because," Victoria took a deep breath and paused. "Well, I honestly don't know, but you have to go home and look at something besides old cheese in the fridge and those four green walls."

"You think I'll feel better if I throw away the cheese?" Fred laughed.

"Not necessarily. But maybe if you get rid of those green walls—"

"I don't know why I'm listening to you. You're not any more married than I am. But I'm ready to try anything. So you're telling me guys don't like green walls. . . ."

The salesman at the paint store gave Fred seven choices of white and the names of three painters who could do her walls in a day. She picked a paint and took all three numbers. One by one she made the calls, and one by one she found the inevitable answering machine. At this rate it would take months to reach anyone. Frustrated, Fred called back each number and left the same message with each service, "If you're interested in a one-day job painting a room, come to 23 Ashton Place and ask for Fred."

When the first would-be Rembrandt in overalls came to her door, he said politely, "I'm looking for Mr. Fred—"

"No, no," she countered. "Ms. Fred. I'm Ms. Fred—"

He laughed. "You're the best-looking Fred I ever saw. I expected some old fat man."

"So did I," she said. "You look about thirty years old."

"Twenty-seven and holding."

Fred wondered who he was holding. "Your wife or girlfriend is lucky to have somebody who can paint the house."

"Told you I'm holding. I'm holding out for the right woman."

Fred felt herself blush. My God, she thought, I'm not out of practice. I still flirt instinctively. "I'll settle for the right walls."

He looked at her and smiled. Such a nice smile, she thought. Some men smiled as if they were walking the last mile. He smiled as though he liked people.

"Why don't you come in and see the room?"

He shrugged, walked through the door, and looked slowly around the room. He had friendly blue eyes. Fred fol-  lowed his eyes and wondered what he was thinking. Finally he turned to her. "You want white walls?" he asked.

She nodded.

He looked again at the walls and then for a long minute at her. "Good idea. You have dark hair and eyes. You'll look really good in a white room. This green is no good for your looks."

"Ummm, okay."

"By the way," he said, "this is a real coincidence. I didn't tell you my name. I'm Fred. So, if you don't mind, I'd like to call you Freddie."

Newly minted Freddie smiled her prettiest smile.

"Want me to do the job tomorrow?" he asked.

"Hey, that would be great."

"But, ummmm, Freddie, I have about fifteen minutes before I have to go to another appointment. Can we go across the street and have a cup of coffee and maybe you can tell me exactly how you want the job done?"

She reached for her jacket. Perhaps Victoria was right. Maybe a woman could redecorate her life if she started with her own four walls.

Who knows what
a coat of paint will cover
—and uncover?

THE WAY WE ARE

Mother moved.

And behind those two words is the familiar story of a family and the kind of difficult decisions many of us are making these days.

My mother has long considered herself an independent woman, fully capable of making her own decisions about practically everything in life. Although the baby of her family, she was the one to whom the others turned for advice, and of course she always had her opinions at the ready for *me*, whether I thought I needed them or not.

My mother, despite two widowhoods, never withdrew from the world; at ninety she had a lively intelligence, loving friends, and two things in her life that made her feel free and independent: her apartment and her car.

Yet even as they made Mother feel secure, they made the rest of the family feel unsure about her safety and welfare. What if something were to happen to her while living alone? What if she were to fall, as the mother of my sister-in-law had, unable to get help?

It was my sister-in-law who started the campaign to get Mother to move. Of course Mother realized it was a planned campaign. The first time Eleanor mentioned to her that there was a senior residence she ought to consider, Mother dismissed the subject.

"You could probably get her to listen," Eleanor said to me.

"I'll have to go slowly," I cautioned. "Mother doesn't buy what she doesn't need." I didn't add, but we both knew, that Mother was stubborn and not likely to accept our counsel. Each of us realized that it would have to be her decision, not ours. And we both knew that now was the time to make the decision.

The next time I went to visit, I decided to broach the subject. I'm sure she saw a "let's get Mother to move" look on my face. After all, she's been reading my expressions as long as I've been making them.

Even before I could say a word, she jumped in. "Eleanor has been telling me to move, but I know you wouldn't do that because you understand that if I have to give up my independence, it will kill me."

But Eleanor had armed me with plenty of information. It was a supervised residence; she would have her own apartment, take her own furniture. Eleanor assured me it wasn't a nursing home, and she'd have her cherished independence. "But Mother," I continued, "Eleanor and I have been talking—"

Mother looked stricken. What was I doing behind her back? "Lois," she began, "this is my home. I'm so comfortable here. Everything I have here is important to me—my pictures, my linens, all my things. Some belonged to your grandmothers and great-grandmothers."

My heart understood.

In so many ways I admire my mother. When my father died, her world changed dramatically. She had always been a protected wife who'd never written a check, balanced a budget, or driven a car. Yet she took charge of her life and learned to do all these new things.

Now, after years of proving her competence, I was suggesting she revert to the passive role she had relinquished. Not only that, I was even reversing our roles. I said nothing more; I couldn't bear to hurt her.

It was a power failure in Mother's apartment house that caused me to realize I could no longer dance around the subject. She lived on the fifth floor, and when the elevators and lights went out of service for five days, she was literally trapped. Only granddaughter Denise's ability to climb five flights and bring food kept her going.

It was then I knew I'd have to insist that she move. Oh, how I dreaded saying what I knew I had to say. "Mother," I began slowly, "if I lived nearby, I wouldn't even mention this—"

My mother put her hand up to silence me. She said nothing for a minute or two and then responded. "I will call and put my name on the list," she said quietly.

"Thank you," I said and hugged her. I'd been prepared to give a speech, but she had given it herself before I could say a word. How like my mother to recognize the inevitable decision and make it for herself. My heart filled with gratitude for her intelligence and grace.

When the next opening occurred at the residence, we went together to see it and were pleasantly surprised to find a cheery apartment with a living room large enough for most of her furniture, a bedroom, and a small kitchen. As we walked through the lounge, people greeted her. "Oh, I'll know people here, but you understand," she sighed, "I'm just doing this for you."

It took five years for her to admit that this was really the best place for her and to understand that maybe the move hadn't been just for me.

NESTING

There are choices we make in life: education, jobs, marriage. Yet our choices narrow as life forces change upon us: unexpected job shifts, illnesses, and deaths. We cling to our choices and try to delay change. But who truly can?

When Mother moved, Eleanor and Denise and my daughter, Kathy, all helped her pack, and I think Mother gave us more than she took to her new home. Now when I open a drawer and see the linens from my mother's hope chest, I go back to my first memories of home. There they are, the tablecloths of so many Thanksgivings ago, the doilies (who remembers doilies?). Yet as I look at them, I don't see the artifacts of housekeeping; I see evidence of times gone by, lives once lived, and I can almost hear my father's voice calling, "What's for dinner?"

A hope chest, like hope, is the gift of mothers to daughters— and daughters to mothers.

III *At Long*

Last Home

GOING HOME

"Going home, going home, going home." The words played again and again in Will's head until they assumed a rhythm, a beat of their own. He almost wished he had a piano; he wanted to hear the music his heart was making.

He tried to lean back in the airplane seat, but it still didn't help. The two-ton man next to him still squashed his legs, and the nervous woman on the other side sent her fearful vibes across the armrest. Well, wasn't going home worth a little discomfort?

It was his father's sixtieth birthday and the relatives and friends were going to gather. "Not a surprise party," his mother had

insisted, "just a surprising group of old friends and family. You'll want to be there, Will?" She asked it as a question, but he knew it was a command.

"Of course, I'll be there," he'd assured her, and he went out and bought the ticket that day. He explained about the birthday party to his boss, a woman only a couple of years his senior but already a partner in the law firm where he had started last year right after graduation. She'd given him a little hug and said she was glad to see him take some family time; she hoped when her three-year-old son was grown he'd do the same.

Will couldn't believe all the work it took just to leave his tiny studio apartment for a couple of days. He had to notify his cleaning woman, stop the newspapers, and look for a neighbor to take his mail. But he'd done it all. Now he could relax and have a great time.

"Going home . . . going home," he kept saying to himself as the plane took off.

He must have dozed because the next thing he knew everyone was fastening seat belts in preparation for landing.

Home, he sang to himself once more as he tightened the seat buckle.

He saw his mother first, her bobbed blond head looking intently at each departing passenger. "Darling," she shouted. He hugged her and shook his father's hand as he balanced his duffel and plastic suit bag.

"Where's your luggage?" his mother asked.

"This is it, Mom. Nothing to check."

"I hope you'll have the right clothes," she murmured.

When they got to the parking lot, Will turned to his father. "Want me to drive?"

"You drive? When you were sixteen, you nicked my fender, and I told you you'd never again get behind the wheel of my car."

"Dad," Will protested, "since then I've driven across the country three times with no accidents."

"Still doesn't mean you can drive my car," his father grumbled.

The party that night, as promised, was a collection of friends and family. "Yes, Will's a lawyer with a big job," his mother announced proudly.

He cringed, "Aw, Mom—"

There were people who began their sentences with, "I remember you when you. . . ."

There were others who said, "I hope you're not going to be one of those big shots who forgets about his family. . . ."

There were those who told him about all the marriages in his high school class, the births of babies, and the deaths of the elderly—and sometimes the not-so-elderly.

A hometown is a collection of vital statistics, Will realized. And we add to them, he thought, as his father blew out the candles on his cake.

"Nice party," Will told his parents the next morning over coffee.

"Did you have a good sleep?" his mother asked solicitously.

"Always the best, Mom," he said quickly.

"You don't mind that we use your old bedroom as a library? You know, they told me at the store that the convertible sofa we bought is even more comfortable than a real bed."

"Right, Mom."

"Did you think so?"

"Sure, Mom. Sure."

"Everybody seemed surprised that you came," his father announced. "They're worried maybe you think you're too highfalutin for us now that you work for that fancy firm."

"Dad, I'm just another lawyer in that place. I'm not anybody important, and I may never be; but the work is interesting."

"Is it a little like *L.A. Law?*" his mother asked.

"It's about as much like *L.A. Law* as we're like *Leave It to Beaver*," Will told her.

"Don't talk to your mother like that," his father frowned.

Will was about to answer and then thought better of it. He looked at his watch. "I think I ought to get started for the airport," he remarked.

"Aren't you staying today?" his mother asked. "I thought you could go to lunch with me."

"Thanks, Mom. No, I have to get back. I'm helping my boss prepare for a big tax investigation."

"You're not breaking the law, are you?" his mother wondered.

"Mom, you watch too much TV," Will chided as he pushed back his chair and went to his old room to zip his carry-on bag for the return trip. If he got to the airport in time, he could go standby on the next flight out.

"But it was so wonderful to have you home with us," his mother called to his disappearing back.

Will didn't say much more to his parents. There's not much more to say, he thought. But once he boarded the plane and waited for takeoff he asked himself: Was my mother always so protective? Is my father angry at me because I moved out of their house and away from their life? Do my parents resent my working for a big-time law firm even though I've just got a little job?

He felt the thrum of the airplane engines. They were about to take off. He leaned back in his seat. It wasn't easy going to see your parents. It felt better now to be wow! going home!

"Going home, going home, going home." The words played over and over in his head as the landscape of his early life slid from view.

*You know you've grown up
when home is where your
parents aren't.*

WHATEVER LOLA WANTS . . .

There comes a time in a woman's life when even too much is not enough. For Lola the time came just after her fortieth birthday, the week she and Sean celebrated their fifth wedding anniversary, the very week she became a partner at Williams, Port, Johnson and Whitbread, the public relations agency that hired her fresh from college. It was also the week that Lola finally admitted to herself that, in the midst of plenty, she still didn't have the two things she wanted most: a house and a baby.

Of course those were the

two things Sean didn't want, and she not only understood the reasons; she had agreed to the conditions before their marriage. She was the second Mrs. Sean Brown. The first Mrs. Sean Brown had been given the house (no mortgage, thank you) after the divorce, and the first Mrs. Brown and Sean already had three adult children. Who needed more?

Well, Lola did, but since she'd had a hysterectomy at thirty, it didn't seem a subject they'd ever need to discuss. So they were married. Both were surprised at the warmth and intensity of their marriage, so sometime during the comfort of their second year together, Lola mentioned she'd like to adopt a child. Sean paused at her words. "I didn't marry you to have a child," he said softly. "I want to be alone with you. I don't want anything or anyone to come between us. I want you. When we married, I told you I'd never met a woman like you, and I'm willing to make you my life. Besides, we agreed, Lola. . . ." His tone told her that would be the last word. The next day at tea Lola confided to her mother that the conversation had been a lesson in human relationships. "I know now," she said sadly, "never to promise away my future."

"Darling," her mother empathized, "men don't always know what's best for them. By slowly living each day and keeping your promise to make him the focus of your life, you will help him see the light. Some women call this The Campaign. The secret is never to be *desperate* for anything, from a washing machine to a gold bracelet to a house."

That had been her mother's first and last word on the subject, but Lola had never forgotten that conversation. For a year Lola followed her mother's advice; she never asked Sean for anything, but she did a hundred little things to make him comfortable—everything from deepening her friendship with his son's wife to making sure they had at least two nights a week at home alone. Over the months she noticed that her mother's observation seemed to be valid, because without asking, Lola had been given a fur coat, a CD player for her car, and various other baubles. Sometimes she asked herself if Sean unknowingly gave these as compensatory gifts for no house and no baby.

And so the months rolled into years. On their seventh anniversary Sean grinned as he took a bottle of champagne from the refrigerator.

"It's great that we're celebrating at home with your parents," he said as he turned to Lola who was carefully stirring boeuf bourguignon.

"Oh, by the way," Lola said, "if Mother seems a little tense tonight, it's because they're going to sell the big house. Dad wants an apartment, but Mother wants a smaller house."

"And what am I supposed to do or say?" Sean asked.

"Oh, just be sweet as usual to both of them, but know they're anxious. And I think, if it's okay with you, that when we go to the Whitbreads out in the country for dinner Saturday night, we might offer to go early and look for houses for them."

When Lola told her mother privately before dinner that she and

Sean would do a little house hunting for them, her mother kissed her and said, "That's just what I'd hoped you'd do."

On Saturday they started their search for the older couple. "This house is terrible," Sean said when he saw the first. "It needs a total renovation. No one could make it livable."

Renee, the real estate agent, laughed. "Someone will," she assured him. "No woman ever saw a house or a man she couldn't make over."

By the time they arrived at House number three, Sean was relaxed enough to admit that the gardens were spectacular and wondered how much it would cost to keep them looking that way. "Too much," Renee laughed, "but if you've got a green thumb—"

"That's not your father. Or me," Sean added quickly.

Lola felt a small excited churning. Did Sean sound as if he were the buyer? At House number four Sean admitted, "If I were in the market, I have to tell you that the gazebo would get me."

"Oh darling," Lola said, barely able to contain her own excitement, "let's not be hasty. But if you like that gazebo, just think about putting an office for you in that room off the dining room. That way you'd have a view of the gazebo any time you want."

"But if I have an office at home, what about you?"

"I could take that little sewing room next to our—I mean, next to the master—bedroom, and it would have room for a computer and bookshelves."

"I could see spending more time at this house," Sean admitted. "Maybe we'd take Fridays for ourselves."

"Well, let's think it over," Lola said. "We'll come back next week," she said nervously to Renee.

"Whatever you say," Renee shrugged.

"Lola—" Sean's voice came from inside the house, "do you think my desk would fit on this wall?"

Three months later, the week after they moved into the house, Lola and Sean welcomed her parents, their first guests.

Sean lifted his glass to toast his wife and said to his mother-in-law, "By the way, how's your house hunting coming?"

"What house hunting?" Lola's father asked.

"Oh, I told the children we might want to move, and then Sean offered to look at houses with Lola, and—well, instead of our moving, they moved."

Lola lifted her glass. "To my mother, the campaigner."

Sean looked at his wife, smiled, and said, "You know, as I look around, I think the only thing missing is a baby."

Sometimes mother knows best.

A MOVING EXPERIENCE

Marta stood and rubbed the small of her back. "I hate packing," she said aloud.

The man from the moving company, his arms thick as steel pillars, lifted a carton of books and grunted in reply. Enough already. How many times had he heard these well-exercised, indulged blond housewives bemoan their fates?

"I'm packing thirty-four years of my life," she volunteered.

So what, he thought. You women are all alike—

Maybe it's better that he's silent, she thought. Maybe these thoughts should just stay here at the top of my mind and the back of my heart. Maybe it's best unsaid. Besides, it all began so long ago. . . .

NESTING

Kassel, Germany, 1944 . . .

For weeks now the Allied planes had flown over the city. No, they hadn't just flown over. As the Allies did in Dresden, they fire-bombed Kassel until most of the city was destroyed. It seemed to five-year-old Marta that the planes moved deliberately down the street where she lived with her mother and the four other children in the family. Why us? she wondered. We don't even have our father here, and we don't know where he is, only that he is a scientist working in Berlin. But after the last time when the bombs had hit their street, someone had moved them to what they called "a safe street."

It was here on "the safe street" that the bombers came again three weeks before the end of the war. And it was here that the bomb dropped that would change the course of Marta's life, the bomb that destroyed the "safe farmhouse." When it was over, all Marta knew was that Mama was no longer with them. "In hospital," her older sisters said.

It was not until the next month, after other children taunted, "Your mother's dead," that a neighbor took Marta into a pretty park. Later Marta would learn that it was called a cemetery, and this was where Mama was now.

149

The little motherless girl was taken back to the house with her sisters. Still Father was not there. By now the war had ended and he had gone into hiding, certain that the Allies were hunting him in order to kill him. Within weeks Father was found, and to his shock and surprise the Americans assured him that no, they didn't want to kill him. Instead they wanted him to come to the United States and work in California, just like Wernher von Braun. And they wanted him at once. He was to get immediate clearance to leave Germany. Clearance was for Father. Just Father. No children. Not now. Perhaps later. The children were sent to an orphanage until other arrangements could be made.

Finally Father was assigned to a job in California, but before he left Germany, he married once again. His new wife took the little

children and moved from place to place until, finally in 1948, they all followed Father to California. The first house in Oxnard was a two-bedroom box house. That's all it was. A box with two bedrooms and one bathroom for six people. But Marta thought it the most beautiful house in the world. It was a house, a real house, and no bombers flew overhead.

But the good times were not to last. By Marta's midteens, her family, now increased by four more children, had to follow Father and move to Huntsville, Alabama.

"Please don't take me," Marta cried. "Let me live with friends. Let me finish school. Let me be." But Marta was now the eldest at home in this patched family. She was the one who could help with the younger half-sisters and brothers.

So she went. And how she hated every day of this transplanted life. All she could dream was that one day she would be graduated from high school and go home to California.

The week she was graduated, she left Alabama and went to live with an older sister in Santa Barbara. Two months later Marta was looking for another home; her sister was getting married and had no room. Marta moved in with a girlfriend and her parents. Within months the girlfriend married and the parents sold their home.

Marta went to the YWCA. In those years, what other place was acceptable for a respectable girl who couldn't afford to live in a dorm? When she realized that her roommate was a dancer with odd hours, she found a room in the home of an ex-boyfriend's parents. Then came another friend's home. Finally her junior year she was able to live in a dorm.

At twenty-one, weary of her nomadic life, Marta married a young man—the wrong man, of course—but he said that his dreams included owning a house of their own. And this house, this very house, was Marta's first home of her own.

The house was to prove more durable than the marriage. Despite their three beautiful daughters, despite her need for home, Marta recognized other needs as well. After fourteen years, she told her husband the marriage was over.

When it came time to divide their California assets, her husband said, "We will sell the house."

But Marta answered, "I can't sell. This house is so wonderful, and we have added so many things that it seems wrong that it should go to strangers. I'm willing for you to have it."

Her husband looked at her and snarled, "This piece of junk? I wouldn't take it, not even if you gave it to me."

Marta felt an old familiar pain in her heart, but for the first time she had the courage to confront her pain and the consequences. "If that's how you feel, then I will take it. It will be mine," she announced.

Over the years she gave up alimony, pension plans, and insurance to keep her house, to add to it, to make it light and airy. It took fifteen years of blood, sweat, tears, and money. Today as she stood packing her past in preparation for her future, the house was just the way she wanted it to be.

It was the perfect home the little orphan in Kassel had dreamed she would have. Ironic that she had been born in Kassel but needed America to give her a castle.

Hard to believe she was going to leave it now, and all because she'd gone to visit her daughter who introduced her to Sam, the widowed doctor in Chicago. "I know you'll never leave California, Mother," her daughter had assured her, "but wouldn't it be nice to have an interesting man to escort you when you come to visit me?"

When the interesting man turned out to be a man she could love, he said, "I can't leave my practice," and she had told him with no hesitation that she would move to Chicago.

Her daughter had questioned, "Why are you willing to leave California now, and you wouldn't when I wanted you to come here?"

Marta put her arms around her daughter. "Because I finally learned that it wasn't the house I loved. What I really loved was the sheltering sense. And you know something, Dear? A man who loves a woman gives even more shelter than the best house in the world."

Once you know the meaning of home, your house can be anywhere in the world.

COME SEE MY HOUSE

We drape the house in hope,
Carpet it with good intentions,
Wash the walls with tears,

Yet only we can see
What we have wrought.

For it is
Behind closed doors
That we comfort aching bodies
And embrace the lonely soul.

THAT OLD GLOW

It wasn't often that Grace's thoughts went back to her childhood home. No, from the time she left Maine until she married and moved to California, she rarely talked about the house where she'd been raised. It wasn't that she hadn't loved it; indeed she had loved it with all her heart. But so many of her sweet memories had been sacrificed to change heralded as progress, and now she feared what "progress" might have done to that small corner of her early world.

Here in California she'd seen houses less than twenty years old torn down to make room for bigger homes. She'd watched throughways rip through residential areas, displacing families. How could a little house like her first home still stand in the face of bulldozers and tax-seeking town councils?

Yet when the university in California,

where she'd been teaching for twenty years, suggested Grace take a course at the University of Maine, she harbored thoughts of returning to her childhood home. "It's not as if I expect to rediscover myself," she explained to her husband, Ralph.

He looked over his glasses and said nothing. Forty years of living with Grace had taught him that she liked the stories she created for herself, and he was not about to become the editor of those stories at this late date.

So Grace went off to Maine, and although she enjoyed her classes, she looked forward to her first day off when she'd arranged to borrow the car of a fellow teacher and drive to the old house. She had no idea what she expected to find, nor did she have a game plan. Once she saw the house what would she do next? Photograph it? Ring the bell? Ask the house if it had aches and pains?

And if the house weren't there, what would she do then? Hold a memorial service in her heart at the site of her first life? Go around town and ask residents, "Whatever became of my house?"

Slowly Grace drove down the old street. Well, look at that! The Grissoms' house was still standing. I guess it weathered progress, she thought, as she reminded herself that it probably wasn't the Grissoms' house now but instead belonged to some family with an unknown name. But still it stood! For some reason that made her heart sing. Not just because Billy Grissom was her first love (weren't they both six when they'd had that mock wedding?) but because Billy's parents let them put up a basketball hoop on the garage door.

And next the Richards' place, she remembered. But when she looked, there was no Richards' place. Instead there was—what was it? A swimming pool had appeared where the house used to be. And over there—oh my, she chuckled. The Burnham place next door seemed to have grown wings. Evidently someone had taken the Richards' property, torn it down (Do they think they live in California? she asked herself), and put in a garden.

The next bend in the road will tell me, she reminded herself. She pulled to the shoulder for a minute to calm herself. Crazy to get so

sentimental over this. She reached for a hanky and put it back. Don't be a fool, she told herself sternly.

She put the car in gear and bravely rounded the corner.

And there it was. Their place. The Coddington house. Of course it probably had a different name now. But it was there. Standing. Tall. Well, not exactly tall. Had it always been that little? She pulled up in front of the house, sat in the car, and let the memories wash over her. How many times had she skipped up this very path to find her mother waiting at the door? How many A papers had she waited to show her beaming parents? How many new friends had gingerly approached the front steps with her? Was the second step (the one she'd fallen from at her fourth birthday party) still a bit higher than the first? Did other boys approach that door as tentatively as her first beaux? Did children go from this house into the world as she and her sister had?

Now she debated with herself. Get out of the car and see if a house is a source of happiness or drive away quickly knowing that the house is there for better or worse? She took a deep breath and made her decision.

Grace was coming home. Not little Grace Coddington any longer, this was Professor Grace Astor. She walked slowly up the grassy path. The trees were bigger than before, but the house now looked shrunken, smaller. Slowly she raised her arm to ring the bell. The people who live here now will not know who I am, but surely they will understand that once my heart lived under this roof and perhaps, in some ways, still does.

Then Grace shook her head and took slow, measured steps back to her car. There was no need to ring the bell and talk to strangers. She could tell from the spic-and-span steps, the little flowering plants along the path to the door, and the tended trees that the home was still loved.

Her eyes filled with tears. At last she knew it was safe to remember home.

*Once a house is accustomed
to happiness, it never loses
that old glow.*

THE CHRISTMAS TREE

Gil saw the tree when he stopped at Chirping Chicken for his take-out dinner. It was leaning against the building with a lot of other would-be Christmas trees for sale, but this one was different from the others; this one seemed to reach its branches out to beckon him. Looks like that tree is asking to come home with me, he thought.

"Hold that tree for me, won't you?" he asked the shivering old man selling the trees.

"Can't," the man mumbled. "Take it now or take your chances."

Gil smiled. How many times had that old man used that line? Well, he'd take it now. The chicken would wait. Besides, he needed a little Christmas spirit for that bleak apartment. Lugging the tree as he walked home, Gil thought about last year. He and Christie had gone to the country and had a tree cut for them. He wondered where Christie would get her tree this year. Well, if she hadn't been so stubborn she could have shared this tree with him. Decorated it with all their—oops—her ornaments. Did she get custody of Christmas tree decorations when they split or were they in one of the boxes he hadn't yet opened?

It was still hard to think of life without Christie. They'd lived together for three years, and then—just like a woman, although she'd promised she'd never do it—she'd handed him his cup of coffee and an ultimatum. If we have no plans to marry by Christmas, you're out of here. That's what she'd said. Out of the blue. Just like that. Marriage? Hey, he wasn't ready. Marriage was a commitment. Living together was an arrangement. They both knew that. Isn't that what they'd agreed would work best? Share expenses. Have fun. Yeah. That was the credo. Have fun. Well, Christie sure took the fun out of things when she used the *m* word.

Gil dragged the tree along the sidewalk. How would he find his keys? Have to prop the tree against his apartment building and then try to drag the tree up three flights. How had Christie done it last year? She'd somehow magically whisked the tree up to the apartment and had it ready to be trimmed one night when he came home from the office. She worked, too, so how did she find the time?

NESTING

⊩⊩⊩

By the time Gil got the tree up to the apartment, he was too cold and tired to go back to Chirping Chicken. Maybe he had a can of tuna or something like that. Christie always seemed to have something in the fridge or the shelves to improvise their dinner.

He opened the door of the fridge. An old tomato. Moldy cheese. Not-quite-fresh milk. No choices there. He'd have to go back. Maybe he'd put the tree in the stand first. He looked around. No stand. What was I thinking? he wondered. I thought if I bought a tree I'd have Christmas. Sort of ready-made. That's how it was when I was little, wasn't it? Didn't Dad just go out and take us kids to buy the tree for the family? We'd put it in the car, and when we got it home it sort of trimmed itself. Easy. Everything with Mom and Dad

163

was easy; that's the way things were with Christie, too. He thought about the house on Millbrook Road where he and his warm little family grew up—the family that scattered after both his parents died. Uncles and aunts lived in faraway places; his married sister and her husband always took their children to visit his parents at Christmas, and his brother had gone to London to work because he'd found a soul mate there to share all his Christmases. But then hadn't Gil thought he'd found a soul mate, too?

What happened, Christie? Why couldn't you be satisfied?

Gil put his coat on, went out into the cold, and half-sprinted back to the take-out chicken place.

Maybe it was the cold wind in his face. Maybe it was the prospect of going back to an apartment with a tree leaning against a window and nothing in the fridge. Or maybe it was just realizing Christmas was coming, and even if you didn't have a home now, you'd had one once. And when they start playing "White Christmas" on every corner, you have to go home.

Impulsively Gil reached in his coat pocket and pulled out his cell phone. The number of the apartment they'd shared was still on automatic dial.

When she answered he said, "Christie, how are you?"

"Okay, I guess." Her voice was cool. Where was that smile in her voice?

There was silence, and then she asked, "How are you?"

"Terrible. I miss you."

"Oh?" Her voice was asking a disbelieving question.

"I guess you're mad at me."

"Not mad. More like disappointed."

"I guess guys don't always do the right thing."

"Please, Gil, don't make this a guy thing."

"Christie, it's real cold out here."

"Where are you?"

"On the street talking to you on a cell phone."

"Why are you out there?"

"Because I was trying to find my own Christmas."

There was no sound on the other end.

He shook the cell phone. Did it go dead? No, the light was still on.

"Christie . . ." he repeated, this time his voice hesitating.

Still no response.

". . . honey . . ." he ventured. "I love you, Christie," he said softly.

Now he recognized a sob.

"Oh, Christie," he blurted, "I was wrong. I thought I knew what

I wanted. But now I know what I really want. Christie, honey, I want you. You see, I was looking at this Christmas tree—"

And then he heard her voice, soft but certain. "But I've got the tree. All I need is a tall guy to put a star on top."

"Wait for me. I'm coming home," he cried as he ran past Chirping Chicken.

Every Christmas begins in the heart—and the home.

A Movable Feast

Jane sat on the steps of the back porch shelling peas. "How many times have I done this?" she asked her mother.

Raina walked out of the kitchen drying her hands on her apron. She put her arm around her daughter, nuzzling her head in Jane's long blond hair. "Oh, I don't know, Sweetie. All I'm sure is that one day your daughter will be sitting in some kitchen somewhere doing the very same thing for you."

Jane looked up at her mother and shook her head. "But who knows where those back steps will be?"

"You're only eighteen, dear. Who knows what life has in

store? One thing I do know. You'll know how to move from place to place."

The mother and daughter exchanged a knowing look. "You mean—" Jane asked, her voice trailing.

Raina came down the steps and took her daughter's face in her hands. "I didn't want to tell you. Here you are, eighteen years old, ready for your senior year at high school, but, yes, you've guessed it. . . ." Raina could not finish the sentence. Her eyes filled, and she put her arms around Jane and moved the bowl to a bottom step. She took a deep breath, and then she spoke quickly, the tone of resignation giving lie to the words she spoke. "We're going to move. Again. Houston, Texas. This should be a good one."

"That's what you said last time," Jane reminded her.

"But I believed it," her mother pleaded.

Jane hugged her mother. "We'll be fine."

"It's not fair for a girl—"

"Don't worry about me, Mom."

"But I do. I don't think all this moving is natural for a family. Sixteen times in eighteen years. But we've had no choice. Each time we've been following your father's career, and they've been good choices. At least they have for him. But I worry about you. You make a friend, and you leave. You like a teacher, and you don't go back to that school. Now we're at your very last year with us; next year it's college. And after that who knows when you'll come home, or even where home will be this time next year?"

"I'm okay, Mom, really I am," Jane assured her.

"Even this doesn't seem natural. I'm the mother, and you're comforting me. I don't really want to move. Not this time, not last time. I'm a homebody. All I want to do is shell my peas on the same porch."

Jane leaned against the porch post. "It came to me when I was six or seven that our family just wasn't going to be the Waltons, and I'd have to learn to find my own way home. So each time we move, Mom, I go into the new place just as if I'd been there before. Then I go to the room you've given me, and I lay out all my treasures. You're

into kitchens and bathrooms, but I'm into things I call my treasures. I have so many. So each time we move I find a special place for my journal and my important books: the Willa Cathers, the Eudora Weltys, and, Mom, I still take the Mary Poppins book that Granny gave me for my sixth birthday. I create little shrines; the year we read *Romeo and Juliet* it was for Shakespeare. I think this next time it will be for someone in the Renaissance."

"I was almost afraid to tell you we were moving," Raina admitted. "I guess I didn't realize you had your own way of coping."

Jane hugged her mother. "To tell you the truth, in the beginning I used to get mad because you and Daddy made all the decisions about moving. I think it was after the eighth move that I found the way to keep my heart from being broken. It was Daddy who showed me how, and he didn't even know it. It was the time we moved to Des Moines; I'm sure because I remember the bay window in that house, and I can still see Daddy standing in the bay watching the movers unload. When Daddy was sure that his twenty-two cartons of books had arrived—he and I stood side by side and counted them—he turned to me and said, 'Well, I'm home at last.' And in that minute I saw how he'd made each move work. He took us with him so we were sort of the heart of home, and then he furnished his life with his treasures. So I made up my mind that I'd do the same thing. I would decide what treasures I needed for my home and then, just like the snail, I could move anywhere because I would always carry home with me."

The heart of home is
a movable feast.

Off the Beaten Path

Tony polished the long mahogany bar as he had for the past seventeen years. I'm gettin' too old for this stuff, he'd told Angela just this morning. Time we quit, went to Florida like my brother. Time we left before I'm too old to have a good time. I don't want to die on this little island running a dilapidated inn like my father did. I don't want to stay in this place where the March wind howls like a ghost looking for a place to haunt. I want to see the world. But how can I ever get out of here? Who would buy an inn with a bar on a godforsaken island with nothing but the birds and the trees? Nobody comes here. He looked around the big old empty room. The whole damned place is a ferry ride from civilization. Why did my father come here anyway?

Tony threw the polishing rag under the sink, pulled the master key ring from its hiding place behind the display bottle of Irish whiskey (when was the last time anyone had ever asked for that?), and made ready to close for the night.

With his back to the door, he didn't hear the couple come in. "Still open, sir?" It was a man's voice. Some kind of accent. Maybe English?

Tony turned. There was a fellow in a big overcoat, eyebrows as big as quotation marks around a kind of nice, open face. Next to him a pretty young thing. Maybe his wife. Could be his girlfriend. They looked too good to turn away. Tony grinned. "I was just closing, but if you want something, I got no place to go except home. And my wife's watching *E.R.* She doesn't care if I'm home late."

"We'll sit at the bar," the fellow said with a wave of his hand, dismissing the possibility of taking one of the side tables. "My wife would like a glass of red wine, and I'll have an Irish whiskey. Neat."

Tony smiled. Thank God they're not some of those fancy water drinkers. When the vacationers from the mainland came over here, they wanted to know what kind of water he had. What kind of water? Good water, dummies, he wanted to say. But no, they always wanted some kind of name-brand fresh-from-the-manufacturer blend. But not this couple. Two drinkers. What a relief.

Tony set the drinks on the bar. "What brings you folks over here?" he asked.

The man unbuttoned his overcoat. "You probably don't get too many people here off season," he reckoned. "We're looking for a place to live. We've been out all day with real estate agents, haven't seen a thing we want to call home. We'd like something—" he waved his hand and laughed, "something big like this."

Tony laughed, too. "You want to live in a bar?"

Now the woman laughed. "No, I don't want to live in a bar," she admitted. "My husband's a writer, and he wants something a little bit away from civilization, someplace where he can work and feel he's not going to be interrupted by all the inconveniences of life."

Tony gave her a quizzical look. "You mean like running water and electricity?"

"No," she continued, "I mean like neighbors and telemarketers and deliverymen at the wrong address and other people's dogs. We want something isolated but with enough room for guests. We've some family who come to visit, and we want them to stay with us— but not in the next room."

Tony nodded.

The man peered through the window at the back of the bar. "What's that back there?"

"Guest house," Tony explained. "This was an old inn, and this was the main house. My father ran it, and those were two guest houses besides the rooms upstairs. I'm thinking about leaving the island though."

The man strode back to the bar. "What did you say?"

"I'm thinkin' about leaving the island. You know, take the wife and go someplace nice, maybe Florida."

"What will you do with this place?" the man asked.

"Sell it if I can. But who'd want a bar on an island?"

"It doesn't have to be a bar," the woman said. "It could be a living room."

Tony shook his head. "How could it be with that pool table right in the middle and this big bar running down the side?"

"It wouldn't be like anybody else's," the man said.

"Why don't you take us around and show us the whole place?" the woman asked. "You do have a kitchen, don't you?"

"With a nice, big professional range," Tony told them proudly. "I make great stews."

"So do I," the woman said with a smile.

"I'll have another drink," the man said. "And now let's talk business. My wife and I like your place. It needs a lot of work to make it home, but we could do it or get it done; and this is just where we want to be."

"Let me call Angela," Tony said. He walked out of the room.

"I'll write a number on the paper," the man said to his wife. "If you think the number's right, and he agrees, we'll take the place."

"We'll have to have it inspected and things like that," she added with her usual practical approach.

"What a place for a writer," he sighed. "I could take one of those little guest cottages at the back, work there, and we could have one for a guest house when family comes."

"Room for our dog and a garden . . ." Now she was dreaming with him.

Tony came back. "Angela says to go for it, but I don't know anything about real estate, so I don't know what to ask for it."

The man shoved a piece of paper under Tony's nose. "Does this look like a fair price?"

Tony shook his head. "Nah. It's not fair. It's too much. This place isn't worth that."

The man and woman looked at each other. "It's worth that to us," the wife explained gently, "so if it's worth that much to us, then this is a fair price."

Tony thought for a moment. "Okay, if you say so. But I think we should do something to make this legal. You know, something like a down payment."

The man reached for a checkbook. "How much?" he asked.

"I think fifty dollars should do it," Tony answered.

"The man nodded soberly. "I think I can handle that without a trip to the bank."

It's been ten years now since the couple stumbled into the run-down bar and turned it into a charming house with a living room that includes a pool table and a bar along one wall.

In this house he's written magazine articles, books, and movie scripts. She has edited major books and has begun writing, too. "When you live like this in a house like this, you have to be a writer," she said.

Never stop looking. Sometimes home and happiness are where you least expect to find them.

Coming Home

If anyone had asked, I would have said, "House? Of course I don't need a house. I love my house. It's perfect." And indeed it was a dream house, the one house I was sure I'd never sell. My husband Lee and I bought it at the time of our fifth anniversary and named it, appropriately, Take Five. After Lee's death I stayed on because so much of our family life seemed wrapped around the place. Even when I was alone, I could look around, close my eyes, and bring back sweet memories.

There, at the stone rail on the terrace, I had posed with my son-in-law Henry's parents and our mutual baby grandchildren. . . . beneath the terrace was the little bush that grew from a plant Heidi, the wife of Lee's son Zev, had put into the ground the week after Lee died. . . . just beyond was the curving arbor and the tiny brick path we had laid from the drive to the front door. Front door—kind of a joke. From the day we first saw the house we never used the front door. Our house was entered only through the kitchen door. It was the kitchen where we gathered, where we whispered our family secrets, learned of pregnancies and the pitfalls of parenthood, drank our morning coffee, and planned our days. Or we could take our cups outside on bright mornings and from the chairs have a perfect view of the stone outcropping that the grandchildren called the Mountain: Each child's first rite of passage was to haphazardly slide, crawl, or climb down the Mountain alone. And dear, brave hearts that they are, each had skidded down the magic mountain by the age of three, each encouraged by the enthusiastic cheers of supportive cousins.

For the cousins, those children born to Lee's and my children, it was a first family house. There was the stone garden bench where they had all been photographed with me for the jacket cover of *Funny, You Don't Look Like a Grandmother,* before running back to the barn where they all lived together, shared candy their mothers never would have given them (but, of course, their grandmother did), and put up signs that read No Adults Allowed.

So Take Five, the jazz musician's phrase for time-out, was intended to be the one house where Lee and I would put down our cares, put up our feet, read a few books, cook some great dinners, and just be alone. But "time-out" was both a celebration and a sentence. Even though we were there for our fifth anniversary, dear Lee never lived to celebrate our sixth.

I suppose I stayed in the house out of habit, a sense of loyalty to our love. And I did cherish the house; it felt like home. The house served me in the same way as comfortable shoes; it protected my walk through life. And then, just like those old shoes we wear, I realized one day that the house pinched a few more nerves than it should. Why hadn't I noticed that the house was really too big, the land too isolated, the life too lonely?

It was my nephew who reminded me that there were other places I could put up my cares and put down my roots. In fact he knew about a barn near the sea, just down the street from his house, and suggested I see it. I saw it and, P.S., I loved it. Oh, it wasn't perfect. Far from it. But I knew I could make and remake this place because the minute I walked inside, the house felt like home.

The friends and neighbors who came to look at my purchase all agreed it would make a good home for me, and they assured me that the house had "good bones." I pledged I would not rattle those bones and try to turn this barn into one of those scrubbed pseudo-Riviera houses. No, I said firmly, I am going to take this sweet place back to its roots and make it just a good old barn where my little chickies can come to visit.

I was ready to go to work the minute the sale went through. It

began with architects and contractors and subcontractors who came and went for the better part of a year. Some of them were very good; some were dreadful; most were competent and kind and eager to restore the barn. Perhaps we all thought that in restoring a barn, we would restore some part of ourselves, maybe that part that gets lost in the E-mail or in traffic on the Long Island Expressway.

The very thought of moving filled me with dread, so I made an early decision to get rid of everything that I didn't absolutely love, treasure, and hold dear. I moved only those things I couldn't live without. Books, of course, were the first things I chose. I took every piece of furniture that had belonged to Lee, added some of my things we had both loved. I took all the art he had carefully collected, and I hung it on the big barn walls along with some of our other things. I built bookcases everywhere the eye could see.

Funny, but as I put the house together I felt Lee's presence. He had always given me a free hand in decorating our homes. So I had no qualms about decisions of color and texture. But there was one thing I couldn't do alone. I couldn't name the house.

All of our other houses had been "we" houses. This was a "me" house, the first house in all my life that I had bought by myself for myself. And even though it was a house where only I would live and my family would visit, I wanted a "we" name.

I needed a name that would keep growing, that would not be bound by a date and a time. I tried, but I couldn't come up with anything. Instinctively I knew that before I could name the house, I first had to make it mine—no, ours. Still, even after I hung his pictures, put his shirt I still wear in my closet, and eased his favorite leather chairs in front of the fireplace, no name came to me.

When I began putting our books in the bookshelves and thought of the conversations we'd had over books and recalled the reasons we'd collected so many of them, my heart told Lee we are beginning to come home again. These are our volumes, a record of life and love with titles only we can understand. Volumes that mean . . . volumes.

There was the very last book he ever read, the one by Robert Hughes about Australia. On a nearby shelf I put the books he'd collected when he was working on the musical *Rags,* volume after volume about the immigrant experience and life on the Lower East Side of New York. Now, like the immigrants themselves, these books are no longer wandering. They are home again.

When I finished cataloging the books, I drove to the beach and, after looking at the ocean, decided to walk barefoot along the shore and feel the waves splashing my ankles . . . volumes of waves that carried the ebb and flow of life, of love.

As I walked along, I stepped on a smooth white stone. Almost opalescent, it shimmered on the sand. How long had it been there? I bent to pick it up, and even though the surface was smooth, I could feel its uneven edges, the hurt and jagged places, the marks of tides and time. I turned it slowly in my hand, and then impulsively threw it far back into the sea. Back to life with you, I whispered.

Back to life for all of love, for all who love.

Back to home where we are bound together forever, you and I, bound by volumes . . . volumes of books, volumes of waves, and volumes of love.

And that evening on the beach I swear I heard the waves whisper one little word. The waves answered, "volumes."

Volumes, the name of my barn by the sea.

Life ends. Life begins.

AFTERWORD

The lessons of life
Are written at home
In brick and stone,
Shingled with love,
Carpeted in dreams,
And interrupted
From time to time
By devilish dreams, chaos, and disorder.

Seeking truths and finding fictions,
We choose the architecture of our life,
Only to change our plans
When we must;
For the lessons of life never end.

ACKNOWLEDGMENTS

The idea of writing about nesting—the cozy and inventive ways we put together the bits and places of life—came to me after my own series of moves and changes. I am grateful to many people who helped me understand that the concept of nesting never changes; only the addresses are different.

Through the years of working on *Nesting,* I turned to friends, family, and associates for stories, opinions, and good times, both in and out of our nests. I am grateful to Michaela Muntean, Patricia Rosenwald, Annelle Warwick Savitt, M. Elliot Schnall, Joni Evans, Robert Wyse, Jane Cochran, Emily England, Marilyn Nye, Eva Pusta, Marilyn Gould, Molly Goldman, Herbert Kasper, Larry Laslo, John Lisko, Phyllis Levy, Helene Silver, Heidi Guber, Katherine Wyse Goldman, Kenneth Wyse, Cindy Greenfield, Hope and Ed Gropper; my friend and agent Owen Laster; my neighborhood bookstores, Bookhampton in East Hampton and the Madison

Avenue Bookshop in New York City; and many people at Simon & Schuster, most especially the editors Constance Herndon and Laurie Bernstein, art director Jackie Seow, designers Ruth Lee and Katy Riegel, Cynthia Hamel, Jim Thiel, and Andrea Au; and a special acknowledgment to Sally Mara Sturman, whose charming drawings enhance the stories.

My loving thanks to each of you, as well as to all the unnamed storytellers, for helping me find my way home.